LONDON
INN SIGNS

LONDON INN SIGNS

JOAN P. ALCOCK

TEMPUS

For Maureen Walshe who has helped to seek out inn signs with the author and also believes that they should be recorded and preserved.

Frontispiece: *Joe, one of the regulars at the Widow's Son, displays the medal awarded to him by the Russian Government for his service on the Arctic Convoys during the Second World War.*

First published 2007

Tempus Publishing Limited
The Mill, Brimscombe Port,
Stroud, Gloucestershire, GL5 2QG

© Joan P. Alcock, 2007

British Library Cataloguing in Publication Data.
A catalogue record for this book is available from the British Library.

ISBN 978 07524 3833 7

Typesetting and origination by Tempus Publishing Limited
Printed in Great Britain

CONTENTS

FOREWORD AND ACKNOWLEDGEMENTS

This has been a difficult book to write, not because of the pleasure of seeking out inn signs but because it has been a frustrating and somewhat sad journey to note how many signs are disappearing, pubs closing to be converted into houses, shops and offices, and pubs being taken over by chains which have no interest in keeping historic signs. Some inns mentioned in this book lost their signs on two subsequent visits. On more than one occasion a sign disappeared between one visit and the next a week later. Indeed. many pubs signs have disappeared and pubs have closed between the recording of the signs and the publication of this book. Many pubs have changed their name several times over the years and where possible this has been recorded. As long as they have a sign, this is acceptable and some new signs are an improvement on what was there before. Some signs are so weathered that it is impossible to make out what they are and they should be repainted.

For anyone hunting old inns or pubs check street corners for these were the best sites for pubs. In the nineteenth century brewers did deals with magistrates to get licenses or floated their businesses on the Stock Exchange to improve or build newer premises. Many London pubs were therefore rebuilt or refurbished during this century. Some became gin palaces with a rather dubious reputation but this transformation seems to have preserved them for their survival into this century. Many still retain their Victorian fittings which are now a tremendous attraction to their patrons. London pubs in particular are sought out by tourists and visitors and the welcome given often enhances the visit. The inn sign is therefore an essential part of the total ambiance.

Some brewers have an excellent policy for keeping and repainting inn signs. They deserve our immense gratitude for keeping up the ancient tradition. Others have creative names but do not have a policy of having signs. Chains of pubs have their own similar signs, which are replicated, and some brewers seem intent on replacing signs with their own logo. This is regrettable as signs are part of a long tradition and also give enormous pleasure to passers-by. It is a reminder of Hilaire Belloc's comment that, 'When you have lost your inn, drown your empty selves, for you will have lost the last of England'.

Given the size of London, it is impossible to cover every sign. There would also be a great deal of repetition. Central London and its immediate surroundings have been covered in some detail. In other areas a representative selection has been made of the more interesting or historic signs. This choice is therefore selective but it is hoped that it will encourage the reader to seek out and note inn signs together with the history of their origin.

I am most grateful to all the innkeepers, publicans and drinkers who answered what seemed to be curious questions; to the staff and customers of the Widow's Son who made me most welcome on Good Friday 2006; to Helga Pihlakas and Barbara Kern who proofread the manuscript and to Maureen Walshe who helped to sort out the photographs.

All the photographs have been taken by the author and remain her copyright.

INTRODUCTION

'No Sir, there is nothing which has yet been contrived by man, by which so much happiness is produced as by a good tavern or inn.'

Dr Samuel Johnson

The earliest known inn signs were used by the Romans to advertise inns and their wares. Signs placed above or by the side of the door in Pompeii and Herculaneum included vine leaves, symbolic of Bacchus, the god of wine, and a bush to indicate a first vintage. This led to the phrase, 'a good wine needs no bush'. There are also sketches outside houses in Pompeii of chequer boards which indicate that board games could be played within. The Latin term, *taverna,* indicated that the establishment provided food, drink, entertainment and lodging. These customs were presumably transported to Roman Britain.

In Anglo-Saxon England the term tavern continued although it seems to have been applied to a mere drinking house. The Anglo-Saxons preferred the word alehouse to relate to a drinking establishment and these were controlled by a succession of laws. Three of the oldest inns dating from this period, though it is not clear whether a name was attached to the inn at that time, appear to be the Bingley Arms, Bardsley, Leeds which claims to date from AD 905, Ye Olde Fighting Cocks at St Albans which has an eleventh-century structure on an eighth-century site and the Eagle and Child, Stow-on-the-Wold which is said to date back to AD 947. Later, when ale began to be brewed with hops, this drink was beer and was sold in beerhouses. By 1550 almost all ale was brewed with hops and the titles alehouse and beerhouse and the nomenclature was used indiscriminately.

During the medieval period, the monasteries provided hospitality both in food and drink and lodging. For the many pilgrims who visited shrines, guesthouses were provided in the monasteries or inns were established at or near the entrance. These had to display a sign as many people could not read and the signs were a means of identification. These included the Old Bell at Malmesbury established in 1220 and the George Inn at the village of Norton St Philip, Somerset, which was established by the Carthusian monks at Hinton Charterhouse in 1397. By the mid-fifteenth century the number of pilgrims visiting Glastonbury Abbey was so great that the monks had a building erected at the gates. This survives today as the George & Pilgrims.

Many signs had a religious origin. The Star was the star of Bethlehem; the Bull might be the *papal bulla* or a sealed document; the Cross Keys were those held by St Peter, while the Salutation showed the visit of the Angel Gabriel to Mary. The Crusaders added the Saracen's Head and the Turk's Head. Other signs indicate drinking establishments loyal to the Crown or the local nobility. The Red Lion was the badge of John of Gaunt, the Bear & Ragged Staff that of the Earls of Warwick. Some inns put up the coat of arms of the landowner.

In the fifteenth century livery companies formed guilds. The Brewers were founded in 1437, the Vintners in 1346 and the Coopers in 1396. All these allowed inns to incorporate their coats of arms or a motif to indicate their wares. The Innholders' Guild was relatively late in being granted their charter in 1515, but they were founded in the fourteenth century and had been given guild status in London in 1446. The government, however, was determined to control places where drink was sold and so in 1495, in the reign of Henry VII, gave local magistrates the power to close alehouses, beerhouses, inns or taverns, that is all public houses or pubs.

At the Reformation, when Henry VIII broke with the Catholic Church, the monasteries were dissolved. There were three results of this. First, the number of inns had to increase to provide the hospitality once given by the monasteries. Secondly, to ensure good behaviour inns had to be licensed by two magistrates who would issue licenses each year. Thirdly, religious inn signs were now rigidly taboo. The Pope's Head became the King's Head, the Salutation became the Angel and the St John the Baptist became the Lamb & Flag.

In 1393 publicans had been compelled to display a sign outside their premises, 'Whoever shall brew ale in this town with the intention of sealing it, must hang out a sign; otherwise he shall forfeit his role'. The result was a huge increase in the number of named inns. In some parts of England an ale garland (a garland of flowers) had to be hung outside the house to indicate a new brew of beer being offered for sale. Before it could go on sale it had to be tested by the official ale taster to ensure both its taste and that it was being sold at the correct price.

So rapidly did the number of inns increase that in the reign of Edward VI an attempt was made to control the number which a town should be allowed. A statute of 1552 reiterated that two Justices of the Peace must license all alehouses yearly. Only forty were allowed in the City of London for example, and eight in York. In the reign of James I an inn was defined as being, 'the ancient and principal use of inns and victualling houses is for the receipt, relief and lodging of wayfaring people travelling from place to place'. In practice the distinction was blurred because all inns sold alcohol of some sort.

The number of inns did decrease during the Puritan Revolution (1649-60), especially during 1655-58 when Cromwell divided

England into eleven districts placing a Major General at the head of each. Many inns were closed as licenses were abolished and those inns that remained were quick to change their signs to suit the new regime. But when Charles II was restored to the throne in 1660 there was an outburst of royalist fever. Signs were quickly erected indicating loyalty to the Crown (the King's Arms) or commemorating Charles' escape after the Battle of Worcester (the Royal Oak).

In the next century the number of inns and their signs increased. There was also an increase in the size of these signs. Gallows signs, which are those stretching across the road, were intended to attract travellers. William Harrison in his *Description of England* written in 1677 says that, 'Some signs cost £30 to £40, a considerable sum in those times, for what was "meere vanity"'. As early as 1419 the Lord Mayor and aldermen of London, alarmed at the size of the signs, had decreed that no sign over the 'King's Highway' should be more than seven feet long. That this was routinely ignored was noted in a tragedy which occurred as late as 1718 when a huge sign in Fleet Street was so heavy that it fell down, bringing the front of the inn with it and killing two passers-by. It was not until 1797, however, that it was decreed that no sign should project in any way to be a nuisance and seemingly this was observed.

Improvements in transport led to more inns being built and more variety in inn signs. Coaching inns put up signs such as the Coach & Horses and the Waggoners. The development of canals meant that inns were built by the side of locks and improvements in shipping resulted in inns being provided at harbours and docks. But it was the development of the railways that had the greatest impact and there were few towns that did not have a Railway Inn sign. Railway mania meant that many publicans changed their signs. This proliferation of inns, pubs and other drinking establishments ensured that there was hardly a subject, which was not represented at some time. Trade, banking, military matters, flora and fauna, historic events, myths, legends and local and national characters all made an appearance.

Loyalty to the Crown increased during Victoria's long reign, when a large number of pubs were built or rebuilt to take advantage of an increase in the drinking population with many being called the Victoria or Queen Victoria. These often had two bars, the public bar where the working class drank and the other, a saloon, where the gentry congregated. Drinks were, of course priced higher in the saloon. It was not until the 1960s that the distinction was removed, often by the simple expedient of taking down the partition between the two, but many pubs still have two rooms even if the distinction has been removed.

It was at the end of the twentieth century that the number of inns and pubs began to decrease as breweries amalgamated or closed them. Pubs became private houses or were demolished for housing. Chains of pubs preferred to have the same logo for every one of their establishments so the local name was abandoned or the pictorial sign removed in favour of just the name or a device so that, for example, Prince Albert became just PA on a black background. Nevertheless there still remain a large number of signs that do reflect the history of the area or have a local and possibly sentimental meaning. Some signs have been repainted to give a modern twist to what was a serious subject. The Three Crowns become the Three Clowns each wearing a crown. It is therefore essential that signs should be recorded before they disappear entirely from the local scene.

LONDON
INN SIGNS

A

Adam & Eve, Petty France SW1. A pub has stood on this site from the middle of the seventeenth century and the sign of the Adam & Eve was that of the Fruiterers' Co. The present sign shows the head of a man and woman, back to back, set against fig leaves and divided by a serpent.

Admiral Codrington, Mossop Street SW3. The sign displays a portrait of the admiral. Sir Edward Codrington (1779-1851) commanded HMS *Orion* at the Battle of Trafalgar. In October 1827 he was Commander-in-Chief of the Russian, French and British fleets at the Battle of Navarino. His tactics ensured the destruction of the Turkish and Egyptian fleets, which left the Turks unable to control the Peloponessos, so forcing them to leave and thus effectively allowing the creation of the modern Greek state.

Admiral Duncan, Compton Street W1. The sign depicts the head and shoulders of the admiral in naval uniform. Adam Duncan

Left: *Adam & Eve, Petty France SW1*

Opposite left: *The Albert, Victoria Street SW1*

Opposite right: *The Albert, Princess Street NW1*

(1731-1804) became First Lord of the Admiralty in 1782 and later Commander-in-Chief in the North Sea. In 1797 he won a victory over the Dutch at the Battle of Camperdown for which he was made Viscount Duncan of Camperdown. The pub was bombed in 1999 but has since been rebuilt.

Admiral Hardy, College Approach SE10. The sign depicts the admiral in full dress uniform wearing the sash of the Order of the Bath. Thomas Masterson Hardy (1769-1839) was Flag Captain on HMS *Victory* at the Battle of Trafalgar in 1805. He held Nelson when he was dying and heard the words, 'Kiss me Hardy', which, since then, have been a matter of debate as to their meaning.

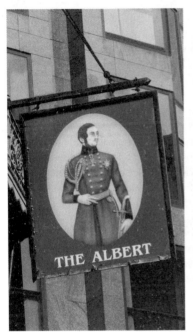 

The Albert, Victoria Street SW1 has a sign of the prince depicting him in military uniform. This pub, originally called the **Blue Coat Boy**, changed its name when it was rebuilt 1865-67. The walls are lined with portraits and photographs of prime ministers from the Marquis of Salisbury to Tony Blair. The **Albert**, Princess Street NW1 has an unusual view of the prince showing him standing with his chest puffed out, dressed in top hat and tails. (*See* **Prince Albert**.)

Albert Arms, Garden Row SE1 displays a portrait of the prince. (*See* **Prince Albert**.)

The Albion, High Street SE25. The name can refer to a poetic name for Britain, possibly based on Latin *albus* or white, a reference to the white cliffs of southern England. It was also a title given to ships of the Royal Navy and a large sailing vessel is depicted on this pub sign.

The Alexandra, Wimbledon Hill Road SW19 built in 1874 and the **Alexandra**, Fortis Green N2. Both show portraits of Queen Alexandra, (1844-1925), the Danish princess who married the future Edward VII in 1863 when he was Prince of Wales. She had a thyroid deficiency and so is often depicted with a choker of pearls as she is at the **Alexandra**, Lennard Road SE20. On the death of Edward VII she became the Queen Mother.

Allsopp Arms, Gloucester Place NW1. The pub was an offshoot of Allsopp's Brewery begun in the area in the eighteenth century. The sign relates to the family tradition that Hugh de Allsopp, who bore these arms, accompanied Richard I on the Third Crusade in 1190.

Alma Tavern, Old York Road SW18 is a Victorian pub, with a mahogany staircase and decorated with delicately painted mirrors. The name is taken from the Battle of Alma (1854) fought during the Crimean War.

The Anchor, Clink Street SE1 was built in 1775 on the site of a previous pub, the Castle and Hoop. From this pub Samuel Pepys watched the Great Fire of London destroy his city. The building served as a dwelling house, a brothel and a ship's chandler until it was rebuilt after a fire in the 1870s. A brewery operated until 1957. It was one of the oldest pubs in south-east London, used by the men who worked on or alongside the Thames. The walls are decorated with handcuffs and other objects from the nearby Clink Prison. The **Anchor**, Lewisham Road SE13 has a sign showing a large anchor on a quay with a ship on the horizon.

The Anchor & Hope, The Cut SE1　　*Anchor Tap, Horseleydown Lane SE1*

The Anchor & Hope, The Cut SE1 has a sign on the wall, which shows an angel holding an anchor before him/her. This can refer to the words of St Paul, 'which hope we have for an anchor of the soul both sure and steadfast' (*Hebrews* 6:19), or it may refer to the spare anchor on a ship, which is referred to as the hope anchor.

Anchor Tap, Horsleydown Lane SE1 was once a brewery outlet or taproom for workers in the nearby Archer brewery. The sign depicts a brewer drawing a pint from a barrel.

The Angel. This sign has a religious origin once depicting the Angel Gabriel visiting the Virgin Mary, the two often being separated by a lily. After the Reformation the sign fell out of favour and the sign depicted only the angel, as does that of the **Angel** in Crosswall EC3. A previous sign of the **Angel**, High Street, SW15 depicted Mary demurely before an angel. This pub was first recorded in 1615 but possibly dates from an earlier period and was rebuilt in 1893. The present sign shows a barmaid, halo above, pulling a pint with a glass of beer beside her. This is akin to the **Angel**, City Road EC1 where an angel, reposing on a cloud, sups a drink. The **Angel**, St Giles High Street WC2 was built on the site of the **Bowl**, which, as it was on the route to Tyburn, was the place where prisoners stopped for their last drink. It is reputed that a sailor named Bawtry refused to have a drink there. Had he done so this delay would have saved his life for a reprieve arrived after he had been hanged. The sign shows an angel dressed in red and brown robes blowing a golden trumpet. Another popular name, which recalled this event, was the **Salutation** and that name was originally given to the **Angel** in Rotherhithe Street SE16. The pub is built over the river with trapdoors in the floor probably to allow smugglers to enter and thus evade the revenue men. Samuel Pepys records several visits to it. This inn was probably established as part of Bermondsey Abbey in the fourteenth century as a hostel for travellers.

Angel & Crown, St Martin's Lane WC2. The sign has an angel holding a crown.

The Anglesey Arms, Selwood Terrace SW7 displays the arms of the Paget family, Marquesses of Anglesey. The pub is decorated with original prints. (*See* **Marquess of Anglesey**.)

Antelope, Eaton Terrace SW1. The sign depicts an antelope standing in the African veldt. A pub stood here before Thomas Cubitt rebuilt it as part of his development of Belgravia. The present one served the staff of the surrounding houses and each class of servants used a bar applicable to their household station.

The Antigallican, Tooley Street SE1 (now demolished) had a sign showing sailors boarding a ship. The *Antigallican* was a ship, which was part of the British fleet in the Napoleonic Wars, and its name was deliberately chosen to defy the French.

The Archery Tavern, Bathurst Street W2. This pub, with its sign of an archer, was a centre for the Toxophilite Society, a group of archers, in the eighteenth century, which implies that the area was then open country. In the nineteenth century the Royal Toxophilite Society, as it called itself, preferred to have its butts in Regent's Park.

Argyll Arms, Argyll Street W1. The pub derives its name from the fact that it was first built 1740-42 on land originally owned by John Campbell, second Duke of Argyll (1680-1743) and whose town house was where the Palladium Theatre now stands. The interior was altered in 1897 and 1900, but still has screens breaking the space into intimate drinking areas. The sign displays the Argyll coat of arms between two supporters (*See* **Duke of Argyll**). The title was created in the Peerage of Scotland in 1701 and in the Peerage of the United Kingdom in 1892.

The Artful Dodger, Royal Mint Street E1 has now lost its sign showing this Dickens's character from the novel, *Oliver Twist*.

The Artillery Arms, Bunhill Row EC1, a rebuilding in 1860 of an eighteenth-century building, depicts the arms of the Honourable Artillery Co. with supporters of pike men in seventeenth-century dress. As this pub is close to the headquarters of the HAC, there are paintings of the history of the HAC, which claims to be the oldest regiment in the British Army as it was formed from a company of archers in 1537, but because its members are territorials not regular soldiers their claim is disputed. Regardless of this the HAC served with distinction in two world wars. (*See* colour picture 1.)

The Assembly House, Kentish Town Road NW5. The name refers to the fact that travellers gathered here before making their journey to the north across Hampstead Heath hoping that as a group they would avoid being attacked by highwaymen.

The Audley, Mount Street W1 has a sign with what purports to be a portrait of Hugh Audley. The pub, built in 1869, has a magnificent Victorian interior, with dark wood and framed portraits. The name refers to the inheritance of Mary Davis and the Grosvenor estate. The story is a complicated one and refers to the lands of the Manor of Ebury. In the seventeenth century Sir Lionel Cranfield, later Earl of Middlesex, acquired part of the manor. In 1626 he sold his interests in the manor to Hugh Audley who held it until 1662 adding further pieces of land. Shortly before his death he settled the bulk of the land on his great-nephew, Alexander Davies but gave the Millbank part to Alexander's brother, Thomas. After Audley's death, Thomas sold his lands to Alexander, but in 1665, 'in a time of the Greate Sicknesse', probably the plague, Alexander died at the age of twenty-nine. His inheritance passed to his infant daughter of six months, Mary Davies, who in 1677 was married to Sir Thomas Grosvenor, thus bringing as a dowry all the land, which now comprises the Grosvenor Estate.

The Australian, Milner Street SW3. The sign displays the arms of Australia picked out in gold. The pub got its name from the fact that it is beside what was once the Prince's Cricket Ground, Lennox Gardens where, in 1878, England played Australia. Mementoes of cricketing prowess are within including mounted bats and wood carved images of Donald Bradman and W.G. Grace. (*See* colour picture 2.)

B

Bag o' Nails, Buckingham Palace Road SW1. A bag of nails usually was the trade sign of an ironmonger but the pub claims to have a different meaning. The pub dates back to 1775 when a tavern called the **Bacchanals** stood on the corner of Kings Row and Lower Grosvenor Street. The original sign showed a satyr and a group of dogs called bacchanals, with the satyr regarded as the devil with a cloven hoof. Bacchanals then became corrupted to **Bag o' Nails** after a play by Ben Jonson. By 1905 the pub was called the **Devil and the Bag o' Nails** but this was soon shortened to the present title. The story accounts for the sign being the bearded head of a fierce-looking man.

The Barley Mow, Dorset Street W1 dates back to 1791 claiming to be the 'oldest pub in Marylebone', and it probably did serve farmers who came to the village of Marylebone from what was then countryside surrounding London. Many of its original features are intact including small snugs and a private bar. The name is more often attached to country pubs as a 'mow' is a stack and as barley is an ingredient of beer, the barley mow sign merely indicated that beer was sold in the house.

The Bath House, Dean Street W1. The name on the inn sign appears in a roundel but below this are two water nymphs splashing each other with waves of water.

Bear & Staff, Bear Street WC1

The Bear & Staff, Bear Street WC2. The bear and ragged staff was the insignia of the Neville family, the Earls of Warwick. There has been a pub on the site since the early eighteenth century; the present pub was built in 1878.

The Beaten Docket, Cricklewood Broadway NW2 is a losing ticket or a lost cause.

The Beehive. There are at least four signs in London. The **Beehive**, Crawford Street W1 was established in 1884. Its sign gives a traditional verse:

In this Hive, we are all alive.
Good Liquor makes us Funny.
If you be dry, Step in and try
The Virtue of our Honey.

The **Beehive** at Vauxhall SE1 and the **Beehive**, New North Road N1 all display a straw beehive. The **Beehive**, a very small pub in Homer Street W1, displays a wooden beehive with huge bees encircling it.

The Bell is a very common name for a pub and one that survived the Reformation as it symbolised summoning people to church. Some pubs, as in Webber Street SE1 and Bell Green SE26 display a sign with one bell on it. The **Bell** in Bush Lane EC4 claims to be one of the oldest pubs in the city because it survived the Great Fire in 1666. It is one of the smallest having but two rooms.

The Bell, Webber Street SE1

Bell and Crown, Strand on the Green W4. This pub, with its sign depicting these two objects has a long history and once was associated with smugglers who came up the river with their booty. The sign may refer to church bells and indicate the loyalty of the publican or the area to the Crown. Church bells were often engraved with the words, 'Praise God, Honour the King'.

Bell, Book & Candle, Ludgate Hill EC4 is a theme pub part of the Eerie Pub Co. chain appropriately furnished with eerie curiosities. The name is indicated on a tiled sign inside the pub.

Betsy Trotwood, Farringdon Road EC1. The name is taken from the great-aunt in Dickens's novel *David Copperfield*, who looked after David. One sign shows her stern-faced and the other depicts her looking down the road waiting for him.

The Bishop, Lordship Lane SE22, previously the **Forrester's Arms**, has a sign depicting a bishop in a chess set.

The Bishop's Finger, Smithfield EC1. This pub was originally the **Rutland Arms**. The sign shows a bishop, dressed in his robes and wearing a mitre, raising his finger. This does not have an ecclesiastical significance, but as the pub is owned by Shepherd Neame refers to the finger signpost, used in Kent and elsewhere, to point in the required direction. The term finger post was a slang term, often referring to a vicar, because in his sermons he pointed the way to heaven.

The Black Friar, Queen Victoria Street EC4. This pub, built in 1878, remodelled by H. Fuller Clark 1903-05, and refurbished in the early twentieth century, is a miraculous survival of art nouveau decoration. The area takes its name from the Dominican friary, which was situated here from the thirteenth century until its dissolution in 1536. The friars, founded by St Dominic in 1216, were known as the Black Friars from the colour of their robes. The trial of Catherine of Aragon, wife of Henry VIII took place in Blackfriars Hall. The whole façade and interior of the pub is ornate with friars imbibing drink or having other connections with beer. The vaulted back room was added after the First World War to provide extra seating space.

The Black Horse, Great Dover Street SE1 and the **Black Horse**, Royal College Street NW1 are only two of many pubs bearing this popular inn sign. It was noted at least from the fourteenth century and presumably refers to the common means of transport throughout history.

The Black Lion is the heraldic device of Philippa of Hainault, who came from Flanders to marry Edward III. It was also the heraldic device of Owen Glendower (Owain Glyndwr, *c.* 1359-1416), a Welsh chieftain who led a series of revolts against Henry IV in the early fifteenth century. The **Black Lion**, South Black Lion Lane W6 has a sign depicting a black lion rampant. The pub was built 200 years ago on the site of a piggery, and it might have been that the pig keeper brewed beer. The long room at the rear was once a skittle alley. A.P. Herbert, the author of *The Water Gypsies* used the pub in his novel but altered the name to the **Black Swan**. A similar sign is on the **Black Lion**, Bayswater Road W2. This pub was first built in the eighteenth century and claimed to be a recruiting ground for the Paddington Volunteers who were formed to defend England against a Bonapartist invasion. The **Black Lion**, High Street E13, a sixteenth-century coaching inn, is yet another place which Dick Turpin is supposed to have used as a hideout.

Black Prince, Black Prince Lane SE1. The pub has a splendid sign showing the prince in full armour holding his sword and dressed in surcoat displaying the royal coat of arms. (*See* **Prince of Wales**.)

The Blacksmiths Arms, Rotherhithe Street SE16 is a mock Tudor building, which displays a sign of a brawny blacksmith striking an anvil.

The Blind Beggar, Whitechapel Road E1

Bleeding Heart Tavern, Greville Street EC1. The sign is a red heart, which was a badge of the Douglas family. The pub was first mentioned in 1746 in the Inn Keepers' Register. A license was issued if the house had a good name with sober life and conversation.

The Blind Beggar, Whitechapel Road E1. The Blind Beggar was Henry, son of Simon de Montfort who was killed at the battle of Evesham in 1265. Henry was left for dead but escaped by assuming the guise of a beggar. The sign shows him accompanied by a nobleman's daughter who is said to have married him in the east of London. The event was recorded in a play, *The Blind Beggar of Bethnal Green*, first performed in 1659. General Booth of the Salvation Army 'opened fire' in the pub with his first sermon in 1865. The pub was also the site of the murder of George Connell by the rival gangster Ronnie Kray in March 1966. Connell greeted Kray with the words, 'Well, look who's here' before being shot through the forehead.

Blue-Eyed Maid, Borough High Street SE1. The name was used in the eighteenth century in a classical tradition as Homer referred to Athena, Goddess of Wisdom with this phrase. The name for this pub is connected with a stagecoach of that name which Charles Dickens mentioned in *Little Dorrit*. It ran between Southwark and Dover.

Blue Anchor, Lower Mall W6. This is another pub from which a view can be obtained of the Oxford and Cambridge Boat Race. A blue anchor has no particular meaning over an anchor as a name for a hostelry, though it may refer to a Christian meaning (*See* **Anchor & Hope**). This particular pub has rowing memorabilia on its walls.

Blue Lion, Greys Inn Road WC1 is not a very common name for a pub. It refers to the arms of the House of Denmark and is associated with Anne of Denmark (1574-1619), Queen of James I and mother of Charles I. The present sign is divided into nine different coloured compartments, each containing a blue lion.

The Blue Posts, Kingley Street W1. Four local pubs are known by this name. This particular one makes reference to the posts indicating the four corners of the hunting ground of Soho. The name 'Soho' is derived from a hunting call. The **Blue Posts**, Rupert Street W1 marks another corner. The **Blue Posts**, Bennet Street SW1 was destroyed by bombing during the Second World War and was rebuilt after the war. There has been a pub on the site since 1667 and in 1813 the poet Lord Byron was a next door neighbour. The blue posts were two posts, which stood adjacent to the tavern serving as an advertisement that sedan chairs could be hired in Bennet Street. The sign depicts the posts on either side of a horse trough. Behind are two men carrying a sedan chair.

The Boadicea, Charing Cross Station WC2. The sign depicts the queen furiously driving her chariot but it is unclear why she is so depicted in a railway station. Boadicea or Boudicca was Queen of the Iceni who led her tribe against the Roman occupation in AD 61. The uprising destroyed the towns of London, Colchester and Verulamium (St Albans) but a Roman army then defeated the Iceni. Boudicca committed suicide after the defeat.

The Boot, Cromer Street WC1 has origins going back to the seventeenth century. Charles Dickens mentions it in *Barnaby Rudge* as a refuge for Protestants who menaced the Catholics in the Gordon Riots of 1780. Leather workers were once the most prolific trade in the area and the name may have been derived from one of their products.

The Bow Bells, Bow Road E3. Though the name of a London Cockney is given to anyone born within the sound of Bow Bells, it is not the bells of the nearby St Mary's church to which this refers but to those of St Mary-le-Bow church in Cheapside. The bow does not refer to a bow, which shoots arrows, but to the bow shape in a Norman arch.

Bram Stoker Tavern, Old Brompton Road SW5. The sign depicts *Dracula*, the creation of the author Bram Stoker (1847-1912) whose novel has achieved undying fame in books, films and television.

The Brewers Inn, East Hill SW18 (originally the **Brewery Tap**) has a jolly sign depicting a brewer holding a pint.

The Brewery Tap, (originally the **Brewery Ram**) Wandsworth High Street SW17 was in front of Young's Brewery, which closed in 2006. Young's delivered their beer in a dray pulled by shire horses. Both the horse and the ram have been found honourable retirement.

The Brewers Inn, East Hill SW18

The Bricklayers Arms, Dartmouth Road SE26. This is one of several punning signs that depict trades. This sign shows a bricklayer, wearing a yellow helmet, bending over his work. The sign of the **Bricklayers Arms**, Gresse Street W1, a small neo-Georgian pub, with a tiny single bar and spacious first floor lounge with easy chairs and a couch, shows a man laying a brick wall. The sign of the **Bricklayers Arms**, New Quebec Street W1 shows a builder with massive arms building what seems to be a turret topped by the royal coat of arms. (*See* colour picture 3.)

The Bridge at China Town, Borough Road SE1 was originally the **Bridge** until it added a Chinese restaurant. The sign is a joining of Tower Bridge and a Chinese bridge.

The Britannia, Monument Street
EC3

The Bridge House, Westbourne Park Terrace W2 is an early nineteenth-century pub built to serve boats on the Grand Junction Canal and the Regent Canal.

The Britannia, Euston Station NW1 is situated within the station. The sign depicts Britannia in her traditional robes sitting by a lion and holding a spear. Her shield displays the Union Jack. The **Britannia**, Monument Street EC3 displays a similar sign.

The British Lion, Bethnal Green Road E1 has the patriotic sign of a golden lion on a green background.

Brockley Jack, Brockley Road SE14. This pub, which opened in 1898 on the site of a previous pub, is one of the theatre pubs of London. The sign depicts the villainous landlord, Jack Camp, also a highwayman when not attending to his publican duties, who preyed on the district and hanged himself before he was finally caught.

The Brown Bear, Leman Street E1

The Brown Bear, Leman Street E1. The sign depicts an upright bear with front paws chained together. It refers to the dancing bears, which once were paraded for entertainment round the East End.

Brunswick Arms, Stamford Street SE1 is a new pub set into an office block. The sign shows a soldier in the black uniform of the arms of the German Dukedom of Brunswick holding a flag. In the background can be seen a cannon with its gunners.

Buckingham Arms, Petty France SW1. When first licensed the pub was called the **Black Horse** but when it was rebuilt in 1961 it took its present name. George Villiers, Duke of Buckingham (1592-1628) was the favourite courtier of James I and Charles I. His meddling in politics led to his unpopularity and to his assassination by John Felton in Portsmouth. The sign depicts the duke in a blue doublet with slashed sleeves and a white lace collar.

*Brunswick Arms, Stamford Street
SE1*

*Buckingham Arms, Petty
France SW1*

Bull. The Bull is a very old sign, probably derived from the *papal bulla* or seal, which was attached to edicts issued by the Pope. At the Reformation the *bulla* was quickly replaced by a representation of a white, red, black or pied bull and this became a popular sign with variations. Numerous **Black Bulls** and **Red Bulls** appear as signs.

The Bull and Mouth was said to have been derived from the mouth of Boulogne Harbour, referring to a battle to take the city in 1544 during the reign of Henry VIII. A pub of this name once stood in Aldersgate and had a wooden sign of a bull standing over a grinning mask with a huge mouth. A pub called the **Bull and Mouth** at the corner of Bloomsbury Way and Bury Place, WC1, was renamed the **Falkland Arms** in 1982 to commemorate the Falklands conflict. It reverted to the Bull and Mouth in 1998 but has now closed.

Bull's Head, Strand on the Green W4. Parts of this pub, with its handsome sign, date back to the seventeenth century and it shows in the low ceilings and handsome panelling. The pub is reputed to have been used by Cromwell as his headquarters during some period in the Civil War. On one occasion he was forced by a Royalist attack to flee to an island, opposite to the pub, and still called Oliver's Island. The **Bull's Head**, Lonsdale Road SW13, with an equally handsome sign, has had its name changed from the **Sign of the Rayne Deer** in the seventeenth century to the **King's Head** in the eighteenth century but fixed on the present name when it was rebuilt in 1845. It still retains the atmosphere of a former coaching inn. The sign shows the bull throwing up his head to bellow in fury.

The Bunch of Grapes. (*See* the **Grapes**.)

C

The Calthorpe Arms, Grays Inn Road WC1 has a sign showing the arms of the family who held some land in this part of London. Some of it was given to the local community for a small recreation area near the pub.

The Cambridge, Westow Hill SE19 is a Victorian pub with a sign depicting the court of King's College and its chapel, Cambridge. The **Cambridge**, Charing Cross Road WC2 until recently had a sign with the portrait of the Duke of Cambridge. Now the sign has the arms of the city of Cambridge. (*See* the **Duke of Cambridge**.)

The Cannon, Cannon Street EC4. The sign shows a trooper by the sign of a cannon, which he is about to fire. Though the name is taken from the street, Cannon Street was once Candelewrithstreet, where candlewrights had their shops.

The Captain's Cabin, Norris Street SW1. This pub was built on the site of the eighteenth-century **Cock Tavern**. There was a succession of name changes before the present one was determined, named after Captain Cabon Norris. The sign is a ship's figurehead of a sea captain.

Captain Kidd, Wapping High Street E1. This narrow riverside pub in a building believed to date from the seventeenth century has a portrait sign of William Kidd (*c.* 1645-1701) who was commissioned in 1690 as a privateer to act against pirates. By 1696 he had decided that piracy was more lucrative and began boarding ships off the east coat of Africa. A warrant was issued for his arrest and he sailed to Boston to seek the help of his former patron, the governor, Lord Bellamont. He, however, refused to support Kidd, had him arrested and sent to England, where he was convicted of piracy. Kidd was hanged at Execution Dock at Wapping in May 1701. On the first attempt the rope broke but he was rehung and this time the deed was done. His body was left on the scaffold until, as was the custom, three tides had covered him. Execution Dock is believed to have been to the left of the pub under the nearby jetty. Bodies of criminals drowned by the tides were then transferred to other parts of Wapping and hung in chains as a warning to further offenders. The last execution was in December 1830.

The Cardinal, Francis Street SW1

The Cardinal, Francis Street SW1. This Victorian pub was originally the **Windsor Castle** but the present name is more appropriate as it is in the vicinity of the Roman Catholic Westminster Cathedral. The sign depicts a cardinal in his red robes and prints of cardinals line the walls of the pub.

The Carpenters Arms, Seymour Place W1 originally had a punning sign showing a rather jolly carpenter at work. The latest sign shows the arms of the Worshipful Company of Carpenters with a wooden mallet and block beneath them. The **Carpenters Arms**, Whitfield Street W1 has the arms akin to the Worshipful Company of Carpenters, with three compasses and the motto, 'Honour God'. The Livery Company dates from 1333. The pub has an interesting collection of beer mats together with its name spelt out in the tiles at the entrance.

The Cartoonist, Shoe Lane EC4 is a modern pub, which houses the headquarters of the Cartoonists' Club. It has a change of sign every year and some of the previous ones are placed on the outside walls. The present one shows a jester emerging from a pint pot. (*See* colour picture 4.)

Cask & Glass, Palace Street SW1. Originally called the **Duke of Cambridge**, this tiny pub is frequented by MPs and the staff from Buckingham Palace. Prints of members of the House of Commons and the House of Lords line the walls. The sign depicts a brewer by a wooden cask holding up a glass.

The Castle Inn, St Mary's Road W5. The exterior is better than the interior although it has stone-flagged floors. The sign displays an unidentified castle. The **Castle**, Cowcross Street EC1 was granted a license as a pawnbroker because George IV required money when gambling on a cockfight. He pawned his watch, which was later recovered by his court officials. The three golden balls, symbol of pawnbroker's, which were originally the sign of the Medici family, hang in one of the three bars. There is also a painting of George IV at the cockfight. There are two signs, one displaying a castle, which resembles the Tower of London and the other showing a cockfight. The **Castle**, Battersea High Street SW11 has a wooden sign of a castle, which probably dates from the sixteenth century and was found during renovation.

Cat & Mutton, Broadway Market E8 is a splendid Victorian pub with a sign showing a cat running away on hind legs waving a leg of mutton in its right paw being chased by a furious butcher. There has been a pub on this site since at least 1680 when the building stood on the Porters' Path, a drovers' road leading to Smithfield Market. John Rocque's map of 1745 identifies it as the **Leg of Mutton** and it has also been known as the **Shoulder of Mutton**.

Cat & Mutton, Broadway Market E8

The Catherine Wheel, Kensington Church Street W8 is a Victorian pub with most of its interior intact. St Catherine of Alexandria (fourth century AD) is reputed to have been broken on a spiked wheel for repudiating the advances of the tyrant Maximinus. As she was renowned for her education she is the patron saint of teachers. The Catherine Wheel is also connected with the arms of the Turners' Livery Company which included a wheel from the sixteenth century.

Cat's Back, Point Pleasant SW18. The sign shows a black cat with fearsomely arched back, obviously aware of some danger. The story is that the landlord's cat wandered away and when it returned the cry went up, 'cat's back'.

The Champion, Wells Street W1. The sign depicts champions in six sports: swimming, boxing, racing, cricket, tennis and golf. The pub was refurbished in the 1950s and the 1980s. Inside are stained glass windows (added in the 1980s) depicting Victorian 'champions' (e.g. Florence Nightingale, W.G. Grace). The singular champion referred to in the name was Tom Figgs, first British boxing champion, who held training practices in the pub, including boxing, sword fighting and cudgels.

The Chandos, St Martin's Lane WC2. The sign depicts the arms of the Duke of Chandos, who was a patron of the composer, George Frederick Handel. In gratitude, Handel dedicated the music of the Chandos Anthems to the duke. The pub has a room devoted to opera prints and is a favourite with patrons of the English National Opera. The statue of a man, knocking an iron ring round a barrel, displayed on the top of the pub had unfortunately been removed.

The Charles Lamb, Elia Street N1 has a lovely sign showing the essayist (1775-1834) in silhouette with a huge quill pen and standing on the open pages of his manuscript, *Essays of Elia*. A silhouette

The Charles Lamb, Elia Street N1   *The Chelsea Potter, Kings Road SW3*

of important London buildings forms a background. He lived for five years in the nearby Duncan Terrace and also wrote *Tales from Shakespeare* with his sister, Mary.

Chelsea Potter, Kings Road SW3. The sign shows a potter bending over a wheel while throwing a pot. The previous sign was changed in 1958 to commemorate David Rawnsley who ran the nearby Chelsea Pottery.

The Churchill Arms,
Kensington High Street
W8

The Chequers, Duke Street SW1 displays the sign of a chequer board. This is a very ancient sign. In Pompeii a similar sign indicated that a game using squares was played on the premises. This type of board continued to be used for draughts, chess and similar games. It was also used for calculating money and gave its name in England to the Exchequer. Some public houses, which displayed the sign, indicated that they would change money.

The Churchill Arms, Kensington High Street W8. The pub sign shows Sir Winston Churchill displaying his famous 'V' sign. The pub is named after Sir Winston Churchill (1874-1965) who had a distinguished political career having served twice as prime minister (1940-45; 1951-55) and who led Britain to victory in the Second World War. His literary output resulted in him being awarded the Nobel Prize for Literature in 1953. The pub displays an incongruous collection of pans and chamber pots, as well as portraits of British prime ministers and American presidents. There is a conservatory draped with greenery, which houses a collection of butterflies. As this pub has an Irish landlord it celebrates St Patrick's Day in style.

Cittee of York, High Holborn WC1. This pub claims to be the latest on a site on which inns have stood from 1430, including an eighteenth-century Gray's Inn coffee house. Parts of the present building, rebuilt in 1923, still date from the seventeenth century and incorporate mock-Gothic features of the nineteenth century. These include a medieval-style hall and carved cubicles intended to allow lawyers to discuss matters in private with their clients. Paintings of members of the legal profession and coats of arms line the walls. The bar is reputed to be the longest of any pub in London. The sign represents city walls, which might possibly be those of York.

City Pride, Farringdon Lane EC1 and Westferry Road EC2. Both pubs have signs bearing the arms of the City of London. The latter pub was first built pre-1914 to serve dock workers but was radically altered to please Canary Wharf office workers.

The Clachan, Kingly Street W1. The Gaelic word means either a small village or a meeting place. The pub, built in 1898, and still with its original fittings, was once owned by the department store of Liberty's and was a meeting place for firemen and police in the Special Constable Reserve. The sign shows a man playing the bagpipes in front of a church presumably as a call to a meeting.

*The Clarence, Dover
Street W1*

The Clarence, Whitehall SW1 (once called the **Duke of
Clarence**), rebuilt in 1862, displays a sign with the portrait of the
third son of George III who became King William IV in 1830.
Probably on account of his royal connection he became an admiral
of the Fleet in 1801. It is reasonably reported that he introduced the
tradition in the navy of giving the royal toast sitting down because
he kept banging his head against the low ceiling of the wardroom
when rising for the loyal toast. The pub, with its bare floorboards
and settles, is very poplar with tourists but it once was frequented by
police from Scotland Yard, and previously served as the headquarters
of the Metropolitan Police. The **Clarence**, Dover Street W1 once
had a sign showing a previous Duke of Clarene about to be pushed
into the butt of malmsey on the order of his brother, Richard III.
Now it displays the royal arms with the cadence of a third son.

The Clock House, Leather Lane EC1 displays a whimsical sign of a clock and the theme is continued inside timed at 11.02p.m. There is a neat sculpture of a lion and the unicorn on the front of the pub.

Coach & Horses, Greek Street W1. This pub is known by the alias **Norman's** after the irascible landlord Norman Bacon who, until his retirement in 2006, ruled the clientele with an iron rod. The staff of the satirical magazine, *Private Eye* held weekly meetings here. This pub sign and those of the **Coach & Horses**, Wellington Street WC2, the **Coach & Horses**, Barnes High Street SW13 (a former coaching inn as the prints inside emphasise) and the **Coach & Horses**, Great Marlborough Street W1 depict a stagecoach laden with passengers. The **Coach & Horses**, Bruton Street W1, with its mock-Tudor exterior, hints at an earlier age. The **Coach & Horses**, Hays Mews W1 has a sign depicting a coachman sitting by his vehicle, with his two horses resting. The white horse feeds from a bucket.

The Coach & Horses, Greek Street W1

The Cock & Lion, Wigmore Street W1

Coal Hole, Strand WC2. This pub was built in 1904 when an extension was made to the Savoy Hotel and Theatre, which had opened in 1894. Coal Holes were favourite meeting places for coal heavers who delivered coal to the Strand area from barges, which docked on the nearby Thames.

The Cock, Portland Street W1 displays a proud white cock on a red background, while the **Cock**, Kilburn High Road NW6 has a handsome rooster. The **Cock & Lion**, Wigmore Street W1 was originally called the **Lion**. The cock was added to commemorate the cockpit, which once existed behind the pub. The sign displays a lion in the desert gazing thoughtfully at an indifferent proud cock. Luckily a ravine separates them. The term cock has another meaning, as it is also the word for a spigot. Inns displaying the earlier sign indicated that they sold both draft and bottled beers.

The Cock & Bottle, Needham Road W11. The earliest signboards showed a haycock and bundle of hay, indicating that the landlord combined a hay and straw business with the selling of beer. The present sign of a cock standing on a bottle would once have indicated that the landlord sold beer on cock (on tap), as well as in bottle for house consumption.

The Cockpit, St Andrew's Hill EC4. This pub probably dates from the sixteenth century and takes its name from the cockfights which took place before the practice was banned in 1849. The pub then became the **Three Castles**, either a reference to **Baynards Castle** that was nearby or to the arms of the Masons' Company. (The pub called the **Baynards Castle** has now become part of the Goose chain and its sign has been removed). It has been twice refurbished and was renamed the **Cockpit** in 1970. Inside the pub are pictures of fighting cocks and these are replicated in the sign. The bar recreates the pit and gallery of a fighting cockpit.

The Colonies, Wilfred Street SW1. When the pub began in 1785 it was called the **Pineapple** after what was then an exotic fruit. It was named the **Colonies** in the 1980s. The sign depicts two people, a man and a woman, waiting to board a ship to go to the New World. To reinforce the message, the words 'The Mayflower' appear in the top right hand corner. Inside photos from the old Raj reinforce the former colonial feel. (*See* colour picture 5.)

Coopers Arms, King's Cross Station, NW1 (now the **Duke of York**). Coopers made barrels and casks to contain beer. The previous sign depicted a cooper at work on a barrel. The sign of the **Coopers Arms** in Flood Street SW1 is as if the spectator is looking up out of the barrel while the cooper adds the last hoop round it. The **Coopers Arms**, Kilburn High Street NW6 shows a handsome barrel on its sign. (*See* colour picture 6.)

Copperfield, Catford Bridge SE6 with its sign of a convivial gathering, possibly addressed by Mr Micawber, recalls Charles Dickens' novel, *David Copperfield*.

The Counting House, Cornhill EC3 was previously a branch of the NatWest Bank as indicated by the tiled floor, the magnificent chandeliers and the gilt-framed mirrors.

The Crane, Armoury Way SW18 has a double-meaning sign. A crane stands on the arm of a mechanical crane. This small pub, founded in the eighteenth century, and once serving the small craftsmen who inhabited the area, has miraculously survived along a busy highway.

The Crane, Armoury Way SW18

The Crispin, Finsbury Avenue EC2. St Crispin was the patron saint of cobblers and shoemakers whose celebratory day of 25 October was also that on which the Battle of Agincourt was fought in 1415. He would find little to remind him of his humble origins in this modern pub set within the Broadgate complex.

Crocker's Folly, Aberdeen Place NW8. The pub was built by Frank Crocker in 1898 who assumed that a new railway terminus would be built close by. Unfortunately the line carried on into London at the terminus of Marylebone Station. The bankrupt Crocker is said to have committed suicide by jumping from the upper window of the pub, a scene depicted on the inn sign. Had he survived, the trade from Lord's Cricket Ground would have made up for the lack of travellers.

Cross Keys, Laurence Street SW3. Although this pub has the forthright sign of two crossed keys and repeats this in a relief of a saint (St Anthony or St Francis) with crossed keys dangling from his waist, a cat at his feet and standing in a river with fishes, the front of the pub contains a motley collection of other ephemera. This includes a heron, swans and cygnets, a bird tweaking the tail of a fox, and for good measure an angel in relief. The inside of the pub has more bizarre features and some good decorative mirrors. The interior is decorated with pop memorabilia including autographed photos of the Beatles. The **Cross Keys**, Endell Street WC2, a long narrow pub, built in the mid-nineteenth century, has the keys of St Peter and cherubs on the front and an interior loaded with pictures and photographs on the walls and pots and pans hanging from the ceiling. The **Cross Keys**, Black Lion Lane W6 may have taken its name from St Peter's church nearby, as crossed keys are one of the emblems depicting St Peter, who is the gatekeeper of heaven. The **Crosse Keys**, Gracechurch Street EC3 was once the banking hall of the Hong Kong & China Bullion Bank, which accounts for its opulent interior, marble pillars, silk hangings and Art Deco lamps. It is on the site of the **Crosskeys Inn** destroyed in the 1888 fire. The original sign of the crossed keys referred to Jesus saying to Peter, 'I will give unto thee the keys of the Kingdom of Heaven' (*Matthew* 16:19). Crossed keys also appear in the arms of the Pope and those of certain Anglican bishops such as Exeter and Peterborough.

The Crowders Well, Barbican EC2 (now closed). The well mentioned here was supposed to have had healing properties. The pub stands on the site of the fort of Roman London and the sign shows a Roman soldier standing by the wall while a cheerful peasant from a later century dips his feet in a bucket of water drawn from the well.

The Crown. This was a popular name for a pub probably because it demonstrated loyalty to the monarchy. The name was totally forbidden during the Commonwealth (1649–60) but soon became prolific once Charles II had been restored. Most signs like the **Crown** at Seven Dials WC2 and in Brewer Street W1 depict a crown representing the Imperial Crown. This Seven Dials sign has a red velvet cap instead of a purple one. The **Crown Hotel**, Cricklewood Broadway NW2 dates back to 1751 when bare-knuckle fights took place close by. The pub also provided refreshment for coaches heading for the North West. The **Crown Tavern**, Clerkenwell Green EC1 stands next to the former house of Oliver Cromwell and is reputed to be haunted as it stands on the site of a nunnery. There are various combinations of the crown with another object as in the **Crown & Sceptre**, Great Tichfield Street W1, the **Crown & Sugarloaf**, Bride Lane EC4 (*See* **Punch Tavern**), the **Crown & Cushion**, Westminster Bridge Road SE1, and the **Crown and Anchor**, Drummond Street NW1. The **Crown & Anchor**, Neal Street WC2 has the crown superimposed on a red anchor. This is also the badge of a Lord High Admiral.

The Crown and Two Chairmen, Dean Street W1 has a black inn sign with a design in gold of two men carrying a lady in a sedan chair, which is surmounted by a crown. Although it seems an unlikely story, the pub may have got its name from the fact that the painter Sir James Thornhill, who is noted for the fact that he painted the dome ceiling in St Paul's Cathedral, lived in a house opposite to the pub. Queen Anne is reputed to have come to his house for sittings for a portrait. The chairmen who brought the Queen to the sittings are also reputed to have waited for her, and doubtless had a drink in the pub.

Crown & Greyhound, Dulwich Village SE21. The name commemorates the joining of two public houses. The **Crown** was the haunt of workmen and farm labourer; the Greyhound was the preferred location of gentlemen who in 1772 formed the Dulwich Dining Club. The **Greyhound** was demolished in 1899 and the site sold for housing. When the Crown was rebuilt as a larger building it incorporated the name of its rival.

The Crutched Friar, Crutched Friars EC3. The Crutched Friars or Friars of the Cross (*fratres crucerferi*) were one of several mendicant orders, which arrived in Britain after 1200. The order was first noted in the Diocese of Rochester in 1244. Its first house was established at Colchester a year later and in 1249 a London house was founded which gave its name to the locality. This was dissolved by order of Henry VIII but the friars are remembered in the street name. A previous sign depicted two friars in mendicant robes, which were distinguished with a cross. The present one shows a jolly rotund friar raising a tankard from a tun of ale. In spite of the name the pub is relatively modern. (*See* colour picture 7.)

The Cutty Sark Tavern, Ballast Quay SE10. This pub was known as the **Union Tavern** when it was built in 1804 but it was renamed in 1954 when the tea clipper, the *Cutty Sark* was given a permanent dry dock berth at Greenwich. Ballast Quay got its name from the gravel ballast that was loaded into ships once they had unloaded their cargo in order to stabilise them.

D

Dartmouth Arms, Dartmouth Road SE26. This pub gave its name to the station on the London & Croydon Line, which was eventually in 1845 renamed Forest Hill. The arms on the sign are thought to be those of the Earl of Dartmouth who began to develop the area after he was partly instrumental in procuring the Enclosure Act of 1810. In fact, they are the arms of the town of Dartmouth in Devon.

De Hems, Macclesfield Street W1 is a Dutch pub built to resemble an eighteenth-century Netherlands alehouse. It often holds Dutch nights to honour national events.

The Devereux, Essex Street WC2. There was a coffee house on the site in 1702. The pub, decorated with arts and crafts wallpaper, opened in 1843 and takes its name from the fact that it was near the town house of Robert Devereux (1567-1601), Earl of Essex and favourite of Elizabeth I, who was tried for treason and beheaded in 1601. The pub sign depicts his arms. Devereux inherited the town house from his stepfather, Robert Dudley, Earl of Leicester, intimate friend of Elizabeth I. (*See* also **Earl of Essex**.)

Devonshire Arms, Denman Street W1. The sign depicts the county arms with the motto, *Auxilio Divino*. A pub has been on the site since 1793 and in the early nineteenth century, passengers waited here for coaches to start from the stables opposite. The present building was one of the few in this area not to be damaged during the Second World War.

The Dickens Inn, St Katherine's Way SE1 was formerly a spice warehouse, which, in 1976, was transported to its present site. There is no sign but the name recalls Dickens' long association with the dockland area, although it is doubtful if Dickens ever entered the warehouse.

The Dickens Tavern, London Street W2 has a sign showing the author reclining in his chair dreaming of his characters that are imprinted on a wall.

Dirty Dicks, Bishopsgate EC2. The pub was named after Nathaniel Bentley who kept a respectable house until his fiancée, according to diverse reports, either deserted him or died on the eve of their wedding day. He immediately closed the room in which was the wedding breakfast and neglected to clean the building or himself until he died. It is suggested that Charles Dickens used this story as a model for Miss Haversham in *Great Expectations*. After his death in 1809 an enterprising publican bought the house and its possessions. The room with its contents was kept, even after a rebuilding in the 1870s, but in 1985 the room was cleared and Health and Safety regulations now prevail. The sign depicts a top-hatted gentleman, presumably Dirty Dick. (*See* colour picture 8.)

Dog and Duck, Bateman Street W1. The sign depicts a dog flushing a duck out of the reeds and the theme is continued with motifs on tiles in the interior. The name recalls the time when the area was hunting country. The pub was built in 1891 on the site of an earlier one built in the early eighteenth century. It is reputed that Mozart and Rossini were amongst other notable drinkers.

Dog & Fox, Wimbledon High Street SW19. The sign with its two alert animals is outside a pub, which dates back to the sixteenth century. In the eighteenth century volunteer troops who practiced on the nearby common used it.

Dog & Bell, Prince Street SE8 has a sign showing a dog with a bell round its neck.

Doggetts (formerly **Doggett's Coat and Badge**), Blackfriars Bridge Road SE1 commemorates the sculling race instituted by the actor and theatre manager Thomas Doggett in 1716 on the Thames, which still takes place on 1 August each year. It is now organised by the Fishmongers' Livery Co. as a race for Thames watermen between Chelsea and London Bridge. The winner has the right to wear the orange livery and a silver arm badge on which is embossed the White Horse of Hanover. This was the emblem of George I in whose reign the race was first begun. The walls of the pub are decorated with paintings of the barges owned by the city livery companies.

The Dolphin, Sydenham Road SE26. This pub is first mentioned in 1733 in the parish register of St Mary's church, Lewisham, when Stephen, son of the publican Richard Peake of 'Sippenham' was buried there. A previous sign displayed a boy on a dolphin, which has been the inspiration for countless works of art since the classical period. Another depicted a dolphin leaping in front of a speedboat. The present sign is a black iron one with a cut-out of a dolphin. The **Dolphin Tavern**, Red Lion Street WC1 has a sign of three dolphins sporting themselves in the waves.

The Doric Arch (formerly the **Head of Steam**), Eversholt Street NW1. A small sign in a pub within the precincts of Euston Station originally showed an engine puffing out steam. It now has a fine sign of the Doric Arch which was built in 1838 by Philip Hardwick at the entrance to the forecourt of Euston station. It was demolished in 1961 when the present station was built. The interior of the pub is festooned with railway and London Underground items such

The Dolphin, Red Lion Street WC1

as enameled station signs and photos. It is a refuge for delayed passengers and commuters from Euston Station.

The Dove, Upper Mall W6 has a sign of a dove with outstretched wings and an olive branch in its beak. The dove also represents for Christians, the sign of the Holy Spirit. This pub dates from the seventeenth century and has Britain's if not the world's smallest bar, only 1.28m x 2.16m. Many writers including Ernest Hemingway and Graham Greene patronised the pub. It is claimed that Charles II and Nell Gwyn used to meet in secret here. From here are excellent views of the Oxford and Cambridge Boat Race.

The Dover Castle, Weymouth Mews W1 has a sign which vaguely resembles the castle. The pub dates from the mid-eighteenth century and has some interesting etched windows. **The Dover Castle**, Great Dover Street SE1 was obviously named as being on the main road to this channel port.

The Drum and Monkey was once a popular sign referring to showmen who had a monkey playing a drum. The **Drum**, Whitecross Street EC1 displays the sign but is now a branch of the London YMCA.

The Dublin Castle, Parkway NW1. The pub shows a castle purporting to be that in Dublin. The name dates from the time when the main railway line to the North West from Euston was being driven though Camden Town and Chalk Farm. Navvies from all parts of the British Isles dug the line, but this often led to violence between the national groups. To try to stop the fighting separate pubs were built in the Camden area. The **Dublin Castle** was the base of the Irish navvies. the **Windsor Castle** served the English, the **Edinboro Castle** the Scottish and the **Pembroke** the Welsh. As the pubs were placed far apart this strategy seems to have kept the peace.

The Duke, Wells Park Road SE26. This pub, once called the **Duke of Edinburgh** depicted a sign showing Prince Alfred. Several years ago the pub was refurbished and the sign now depicts John Wayne, 'the duke', resplendent in cowboy gear and hat. (*See* colour picture 9.)

Duke of Albemarle, Stafford Street W1. This pub appears to be undergoing a transformation but it originally had a sign with a portrait of the duke. The name commemorates George Monck (1608-70), who joined the Cromwellian parliamentary army in 1646 and in 1650 took command of Col. Monck's Regiment of Foot as part of the New Model Army. After the death of Oliver Cromwell in 1658, Monck became convinced that the Republic and the Commonwealth (1649-58) could not survive under Oliver's son, Richard Cromwell. He marched his army from the small town of Coldstream on the English-Scottish border to London and was largely responsible for securing the election of a new parliament which immediately invited Charles II to resume the throne of

England. The grateful monarch created Monck, the first Duke of Albemarle and his soldiers immediately became personal guards to the sovereign. The mounted troops merged into the Life Guards but after Monck's death the foot soldiers of his regiment were granted the title of the Coldstream Guards.

Duke of Argyll, Brewer Street W1. The sign depicts a splendid coat of arms of the duke with his motto, *Ne Obliviscaris*. The Marquis of Lorne married Princess Louise, fourth daughter of Queen Victoria, in 1871 but did not become the 9th Duke of Argyll until 1900. Between 1878-83 he was Governor General of Canada. (*See* **Argyll Arms**.)

The Duke of Cambridge, St Peter's Street N1 has a sign showing a half portrait of the duke. The duke (1819-1904) was a first cousin of Queen Victoria and Commander-in-Chief of the British Army (1856-95) who constantly obstructed progress of the army towards modification and as a fighting machine. This did not prevent his name being attached to numerous pubs.

Duke of Cumberland, New Kings Road SW6 was originally the **Dukes Head**. William Augustus (1721-65), second son of George II had a distinguished military career, especially in the Netherlands during the War of the Austrian Succession and who won the Battle of Culloden (1746). His reputation was blighted by his bloody repression of the Highlands after the battle.

The Duke of Hamilton, New End NW3 refers to the first Duke of Hamilton (1606-49) who was advisor to Charles I on Scottish affairs. He fought for Charles at the Battle of Preston in 1648, was captured and beheaded.

Duke of Kendal. This pub, with its sign depicting the duke on horseback, in Connaught Street W2 recalls the name of a once lesser-known member of the royal family, Prince Leopold, who was the husband of

Princess Charlotte. When Belgium secured her independence in 1830 he accepted the throne, becoming her first King.

The Duke of Kent, Scotch Common W13. This is a huge pub with fine chandeliers hanging from domed windows. The Duke of Kent, depicted in army uniform on the sign, was a brother of William IV and the father of Queen Victoria.

Duke of St Albans, Highgate Road NW5. Charles Beauclerk, the illegitimate son of Charles II by Nell Gwyn, was created Duke of St Albans.

The Duke of Sussex, Baylis Road SE1 has two signs. One shows a portrait of the duke wearing the Garter Star; the other depicts a regimental shako and a sword. Frederick (1773-1843), the sixth son of George III, was created Duke of Sussex in 1801. He died without issue and the title became extinct.

Duke of Wellington (*See* also the **Wellington**). This is a very popular inn sign. Arthur Wellesley (1769-1852), created first Duke of Wellington, had a distinguished career in India before he defeated the French troops in Spain and at the Battle of Waterloo in 1815. He entered politics and was prime minister from 1828-30, although his reactionary views almost led to civil unrest. On his death he was given a grand state funeral, and is buried in St Paul's Cathedral. The **Duke of Wellington**, Eaton Terrace SW1 portrays the duke in the manner of the famous Goya portrait. The **Duke of Wellington**, Crawford Street W1 calls itself a village pub, with its inside decorated with military memorabilia. The sign of the **Duke of Wellington**, Toynbee Street E1 shows a portrait of the duke on one side of its sign and somberly surveying the battlefield with his troops deployed behind him on the other. The **Duke of Wellington**, Portobello Road W11 has two signs: one displays a portrait of the duke with a pair of wellington boots behind him; the other has the duke's head on top of a wellington boot. (*See* also the **Wellington** and colour picture 10.)

The Duke of York, Clerkenwell Road EC1

Duke of York. This sign usually refers to Frederick Augustus (1763-1827), second son of George III who commanded the English army during a campaign in Flanders in 1794. He has had the misfortune to be vilified as the Grand Old Duke of York who led 10,000 men to the top of the hill and marched them down again which is a fallacy as the duke was then commanding an army of 30,000 men in one of the flattest areas in Europe. The **Duke of York** in Borough Road SE1 became the **Goose and Firkin** when it was taken over by the Firkin Brewery, but as the original pub sign was carved above the door this could not be removed and so it was retained when the pub reverted to its original name. There is now an additional sign depicting the duke in eighteenth-century army uniform. The **Duke of York** in Clerkenwell Road EC1 depicts the duke in the robes of the Garter and the **Duke of York** in Edgware Road shows head and shoulders in profile in civilian dress with top hat but still wearing the Order of the Garter. The **Duke of York** in Victoria Street SW1, built in 1821, originally called the **Royal Standard**, shows the head and shoulders of the duke with military hat and cloak. The best signs are probably those for the **Duke of York** in Charlotte Place W1, an interesting small pub, where the hanging sign shows the duke in civilian clothing but the large board has the duke riding into battle leading his soldiers in their distinctive red coats and flying the Union Jack as they march towards the enemy. The **Duke of York**, King's Cross Station NW1 (formerly the **Coopers**) depicts the badge of the white rose of York, presumably suitable for a station which has a train service to York.

The Duke's Head, Lower Richmond Road, SW15, is a splendid viewing point for the start of the Oxford and Cambridge Boat Race, which began in 1829. The present pub dating from the mid-nineteenth century and refurbished in 1894, still retains many original features including embossed glass and mahogany panelling, and has a sign showing an unknown duke, who is somewhat similar to the Duke of Monmouth. James Fitzroy, reputedly an illegitimate son of Charles II and Lucy Walters, was created Duke of Monmouth in 1663. On the death of Charles he raised a rebellion in the South West to claim the throne. He was defeated at the Battle of Sedgemoor in 1685 and was executed in London.

Dulwich Wood House, Sydenham Hill SE26, with its outline sign of a house, through which leads a road between meadows, recalls the area when part of Westwood Common. It was originally a private house designed by Sir Joseph Paxton, the creator of the nearby Crystal Palace. The glass palace was moved from Hyde Park after the 1851 Exhibition to Sydenham, but then gave its name to the area. Paxton came to live in a house nearby and designed other houses in the surrounding area. This house became a pub in 1889 but still retains the atmosphere of a comfortable middle-class home.

E

Eagle. This sign was a popular one as it referred to St John the Evangelist. As such it was used to ornament a lectern on which the bible was placed. The Romans used it to decorate a military standard. Pub signs may have indicated a reference to St John but this connotation was rejected at the Reformation. The most famous **Eagle** in London is the one in Shepherdess Walk EC1, built on the site of a former music hall, where the sign depicts an eagle with wings outspread in flight. The pub is remembered in the rhyme:

> Up and down the City Road,
> In and out the Eagle,
> That's the way the money goes,
> Pop goes the weasel.

This seems to refer to popping or pawning the weasel, a slang name for an iron, a household object that could be easily be pawned when the family was short of money. It alludes to cockney rhyming slang, weasel and stoat (coat).

Earl of Camden, Camden Street NW1 has the earl portrayed in full-bottomed wig. Sir Charles Pratt (1714-94) became first Baron Camden in 1765 and then first Earl Camden in 1786. He was an excellent Lord Chief Justice being a leading exponent for civil liberties in eighteenth-century England. Through marriage he

The Eagle, Shepherdess Walk
EC1

acquired a considerable area including Kentish Town, which he began to develop, thus laying the foundations of Camden Town later leased out for housing. The name came from his Chislehurst estate, Camden Place.

The Earl of Essex, Danbury Street N1. The pub was named after the favourite courtier of Elizabeth I. (*See* the **Devereux**.)

East India Arms, Fenchurch Street EC3. The sign depicts the arms of the East India Co. with its distinctive three sailing ships commemorating the trade, which came from the Far East. Elizabeth I chartered the company in 1600 to establish trade with the East, especially India. After Robert Clive's victories (1751-57) it became virtual ruler in India, which lasted until the British government assumed direct control of India in 1858. The company was dissolved in 1874.

Eight Bells, Fulham High Street SW6

The Edgar Wallace, Essex Street WC2 was named after the writer (1875-1932) who wrote 175 thrillers, 957 short stories and also film scripts for Hollywood, including *King Kong*. He had previously been a ship's cook, and an orderly in the Royal Army Medical Corps before becoming a journalist. The pub prior to 1975 was known as **The Essex Head**, a name inherited from an older inn on the site and near to Essex House. The walls are covered with Wallace memorabilia. (*See* the **Devereux**.)

Edinboro Castle, Mornington Terrace NW1. The sign shows the castle in Edinburgh. (*See* the **Dublin Castle**.)

Eight Bells, Fulham High Street SW6, which dates from the eighteenth century, with its appropriate sign of eight bells may refer to the usual eight bells rung in a peal or to the eight bells that end a naval watch. The interior contains pictures of ships and the river Thames.

Elephant and Castle. The name may refer to the crest of the Worshipful Company of Cutlers, whose grant of arms dates from 1476, which has an elephant with a howdah on its back. Another suggestion is that it is a corruption of the name of the *Infanta de Castile*, referring to Eleanor of Castile, the first wife of Edward I, King of England, 1272-1307. When she died in the North of England, Edward brought back her body for burial in London. Each night where the body rested a cross was built. The last one was outside Westminster at the village of Charing, hence the name Charing Cross. A nineteenth-century replacement cross stands in the forecourt of the station. The **Elephant and Castle**, SE1 was first mentioned in 1765 and became a busy coaching inn serving the southeast. It was twice rebuilt before being demolished in 1959 when the present shopping complex was built. By then the pub had given its name to the area where five busy roads meet. A newly built pub has a small golden-coloured elephant for its sign. When the shopping centre was built the huge pink elephant with a howdah on its back in the form of a crenellated castle was placed on top of the entrance. The howdah appears on the pub sign of the **Elephant** in Fenchurch Street EC3. Sitting in it is a European wearing a large topee and in front sits the Indian guide.

Emma Hamilton, Kingston Road SW20 with its portrait sign commemorates Lady Hamilton (1765-1815), wife of Sir William Hamilton, who became mistress of Horatio Nelson after 1798. They had a daughter in 1801. (*See* colour picture 11.)

The Engineer, Gloucester Avenue NW1 has a sign showing Isambard Kingdom Brunel in his characteristic top hat, smoking a cigar and standing before his creation of the Tamar Bridge.

The Enterprise, Haverstock Hill NW3 displays the sign of an Eskimo being offered an ice cream by an enterprising vendor in the middle of a polar region. This is not surprising given that next door is Marine Ices. Other pubs with this name refer to that of a

*The Enterprise, Haverstock
Hill NW8*

steam-driven omnibus, which was used in the 1830s by the London
& Paddington Steam Carriage Co.

The Euston Flyer, Euston Road, NW1. The sign depicts a red-painted
engine. There seems to be no locomotive associated with the name so
the pub was probably named because of its proximity to Euston.

Exmouth Arms, Starcross Street NW1. The pub dates back to
about 1815, although it was rebuilt a hundred years later. Sir Edward
Pellew (1787-1833) was created Lord Exmouth after he won a naval
victory against the Barbary Coast pirates at Algiers in 1818. The sign
bears his arms. Starcross Street was named after the village near his
birthplace at Exmouth.

F

The Falcon, St John's Hill SW11, a Victorian pub, but probably dating back to the eighteenth century has the sign of a huge bird flying down to pounce. A falcon was the crest of the St John family who were Lords of the Manor of Battersea.

The Feathers, Broadway SW1. (*See* **Prince of Wales**.)

The Ferry House, Ferry Street E14, dating from 1823, is reputed to be the oldest pub on the Isle of Dogs. The name comes from the fact that it was the ferry-master's house but before that a pub was said to have been on the site since the sixteenth century.

The Fitzroy Tavern, Charlotte Street W1, which claims to have given its name to the district of Fitzrovia, was once the local of such diverse characters as George Orwell, Dylan Thomas, the hangman Albert Pierrepoint, the painter Walter Sickert and Coco the Clown. The pub, built in 1897, contains much dark mahogany. The pub takes its name from Henry Fitzroy, the illegitimate son of Charles II and Barbara, Duchess of Cleveland. He was created Earl of Euston, a title taken from the estates of the wife he was forced to marry when he was nine and she was five. Later he was created Duke of Grafton. The coat of arms is the royal coat of arms in the time of Charles II but without the bar sinister and with a greyhound as a supporter instead of a unicorn. (*See* colour picture 12 and **The Grafton Arms**.)

The Flask, Flask Walk NW3

Flowers of the Forest, Westminster Bridge Road SE1

The Flask, Flask Walk NW3 dates back to 1663. The sign shows a thirsty soldier drinking from his flask. The pub was originally called the **Thatched House** and then the **Lower Flask**. There was an **Upper Flask**, which has now been demolished. Mineral waters, which were discovered in the vicinity, were exploited for their presumed medicinal qualities and flasks of this mineral water could be bought at the pub. The present building dates from a rebuilding of 1874 intended to serve the local workers and at one time had separate bars dividing the gentry from the working class.

Flowers of the Forest, Westminster Bridge Road, SE1, although a modern nondescript pub, has an interesting sign depicting a piper in modern dress, wearing a uniform akin to that of the Scots Guards, and in the background a shadowy soldier with shield and claymore

dressed as if in the eighteenth century. The *Flowers of the Forest* is a
lament said to have been composed and played by a single piper on
9 September 1514 when James IV of Scotland and the flower of the
Scottish nobility were killed at the Battle of Flodden.

The Flying Dutchman, Wells Way SE5 commemorates the
legendary story of Vanderdecken, a Dutch captain, who had sworn
by all the devils in hell that he would round the Cape of Good
Hope, regardless of the weather until the Day of Judgement. The
Devil took him at his word and he was fated to sail the seas until
the Last Judgment unless redeemed by a woman's love. The tale is
immortalised in Wagner's opera, *The Flying Dutchman*.

The Flying Horse, Sun Street EC2. As the sign makes clear the
winged horse is Pegasus ridden, according to Greek mythology, by
Bellerophon. It was also the heraldic device of the Knights Templar.

Founders Arms, Hopton Street SE1 is a pleasant pub alongside
the Thames in front of the Tate Modern. The sign is a mock-up coat
of arms, which includes a foundry topped with flames.

Fountains Abbey, Praed Street W2. The name has no connection
with the great abbey in Yorkshire. The sign shows an arch and under

Fountains Abbey, Praed Street W2

Fox & Anchor,
Charterhouse Street EC1

it a fountain with water springing from a base, which refers to the local springs and wells in the area. The name also commemorates a connection with Westminster Abbey, which owned the Manor of Paddington during the Saxon period. The pub boasts that it was the mould spores from the beer in this pub which blew through the windows of Sir Alexander Fleming's office and once collected, enabled him to make the breakthrough in 1928 to discover the uses of penicillin.

Fox & Anchor, Charterhouse Street EC1. This pub was built in 1898 and retains its terracotta façade incorporating a vignette of a fox and anchor at the top. The overhanging sign shows a fox rearing up at an anchor. The interior has a long bar and several small booths.

Fox & Hounds. This is a popular inn sign even in London. The **Fox & Hounds** in Passmore Street SW1, which until 1990 limited itself to selling only beer, also limits itself to three hounds but the **Fox & Hounds** sign in Kirkdale SE26 shows the hunt in full cry as does the **Fox & Hounds**, Besson Street SE14.

The Fox & Pheasant, Billing Road SW10. Originally the **Bedford Arms** this is a simple pub with a sign indicating its rural origins of a fox waiting to pounce on a pheasant. The pub retains its small booths and some original stained glass.

Fox on the Hill, Denmark Hill SE5. The sign displays an obvious scene. This pub, built in 1954, replaced the **Fox under the Hill** destroyed by a landmine in 1941. The hunting element for the last pub was chosen because George, Prince of Denmark, husband of Queen Anne had a hunting lodge in the area.

The Freemasons Arms, Long Acre WC2 is within sight of the Freemasons Hall built in Art Deco style and housing the Grand Lodge of England and the principal meeting place for Masonic lodges in London. The inn sign depicts a coat of arms. There are also the **Freemason's Arms**, Downshire Hill NW3 and the **Freemasons**, Northside SW18 both having excellent signs. During the Medieval period the freemasons were stonemasons who organised their members into a guild which trained apprentices into a craft. They were careful about whom they admitted to the trade. The modern freemasons are members of a fraternal society.

French House, Dean Street W1. The sign depicts three fleurs-de-lis on a shield surmounted by two French flags and the Cross of Lorraine. The motto, not surprisingly, is *Liberté*, *Égalité*, and *Fraternité*. Originally this pub was known as the **York Minister** but it changed it name during the Second World War when Free French troops and the French Resistance adopted it as their base. It

Friend at Hand, Herbrand Street WC1

is reputed that Charles de Gaulle wrote his historic defiance to the Nazis in an upper room. In the 1950s it was patronised by the artistic elements of Bohemia including Dylan Thomas and Francis Bacon. The interior is covered with theatrical memorabilia.

Friend at Hand, Herbrand Street WC1. The original sign of this pub was a lifeboat man stretching out his hand to a drowning sailor. The present one shows a St Bernard dog coming across the snow to a man buried up to his neck in snow and feebly reaching out both hands for help, presumably to reach the barrel round the neck of the dog.

G

The **George** is a popular name for a pub originally referring to St George, the patron saint of England. It has been suggested that there may have been almost fifty pubs with this name in London, but it can refer to the kings of England. Some signs, such as that in Wardour Street W1, depict George of Hanover who became George I, King of England in 1714, following the death of the last Stuart, Queen Anne. The majority of signs bear an image of George III (1760-1820), such as that in Great Queen Street WC2. The **George**, Strand WC2 has two signs, the one on the façade depicting George in his coronation robes. Unfortunately for royalists the pub was named after its first owner, George Simpkins. This apparently Gothic building was founded as a coffee house in 1723 and became the **George Hotel** in 1820. Amongst those who patronised it were Samuel Johnson and Oliver Goldsmith. It was rebuilt in the nineteenth century with Gothic features, but intriguingly has details of frogs, monks and naked men chasing pigs and geese on the façade. The **George**, D'Arblay Street W1 is a late Victorian pub with many original features. The exterior is composed of bands of red brick and white stone that culminate in what may be a portrait of George IV. The **George IV**, Portugal Street WC2 is owned by the London School of Economics but it welcomes the general public. The sign more decidedly portrays the king. The **George Inn**, Borough High Street SE1 is the only remaining galleried inn in London and the present inn probably dates from 1667. The outer galleries are the

The George, Great Queen Street WC2

only means of getting from one room to the next. It was originally called the **St George & Dragon** and as such is marked on a map of 1542 and on John Rocques' map of 1746. The National Trust states that the present inn was built in 1677 and that it is the last galleried inn left in London. In the early nineteen the century at least a hundred coaches a week departed regularly mainly to Sussex and Kent. Wagons did likewise and post-chaises could be hired. Passengers usually waited in what is now known as the Old Bar. Charles Dickens was a regular visitor and mentions the inn in *Little Dorrit*. The central and south wings were demolished in 1895 and in the 1930s there were proposals to demolish the rest, so the National Trust bought it in 1937 to ensure its preservation. There are three signs. The one at the main entrance depicts St George on horseback in full armour rearing up to fight the dragon. The second does likewise. The third in the farthest corner of the courtyard depicts a fresh-faced St George wearing armour and holding a lance and a shield on which is the distinctive red cross. (*See* colour picture 13.)

George & Dragon, Cleveland Street W1. The hanging sign depicts a huge green dragon rearing up to fight St George, but the sign on the wall shows the saint driving his lance into the defeated dragon. The sign of the **George & Dragon**, Lewisham Road SE10 shows the armoured St George driving a lance into the body of the dragon which lies helpless on its back. St George is the patron saint of England who has no distinctive connection with England. There are two suggestions as to his origin. George of Cappadocia was described by the historian Edward Gibbon as, 'an energetic and unscrupulous pork contractor', yet he became the Arian Bishop of Alexandria (AD 356-61). As churches had already been dedicated to him in the Near East some fifty years earlier, the original St George therefore seems to have been a soldier from Lydda in Palestine, who was martyred during the reign of the Roman Emperor Diocletian about AD 303. His cult came into England when Richard I (1189-99), who had had a vision assuring him of the saint's protection, encouraged the knights who accompanied him on the Third Crusade to wear a surcoat of a red cross on a white background and to dedicate themselves to St George. Edward III (1327-77) named him as England's patron saint and in 1344 founded the order of the Garter with St George on its badge. St George's name became a rousing battle cry as recalled by Shakespeare in *Henry V*, 'Cry God for Harry! England and Saint George' (*Henry V*, Act 3, sc. 1, l. 31). The dragon was added as a symbol of the fight between good and evil but *The Golden Legend* says that St George saved the life of a princess who was about to be sacrificed in order to propitiate a dragon, who had terrorised the country. St George defeated the dragon whereupon many people hastened to be baptised and reject their cruel ways. The legend therefore represents the triumph of good over evil and as such the Church promulgated it. His feast day is 23 April.

George and Vulture, St Michael's Alley EC3. The sign of this small pub shows what appears to be a double-headed eagle rather than a vulture, set against the cross of St George. The pub was originally called the **George**, but got its present name from a tethered live vulture owned by a wine merchant who used it as an advertisement.

Gipsy Moth, Greenwich Church Street SW10 was originally the **Wheatsheaf**. In 1975 its name was changed to commemorate the single-handed voyage round the world in his yacht, *Gipsy Moth*, by Sir Francis Chichester (1901-72). When he arrived at Greenwich, he was knighted by the Queen.

Gipsy Tavern, Gypsy Road SE19 has an appropriate sign showing a gipsy relaxing outside her caravan while her son holds a horse. The sign of the **Gipsy Hill Tavern**, Gypsy Hill SE19 shows a gipsy telling a lady's fortune while her male companion looks indulgently on. The area was once home to gipsies who came to fairs held on Westwood Common in the Sydenham area.

The Gladstone Arms, Lant Street SE1 has a sign of a portrait of the young William Ewart Gladstone (1809-98), while the

The Gladstone Arms, Lant Street SE1

The Glassblower, Glasshouse Street W1

Gladstone, Portland Road SE25 has a sign showing an elderly Gladstone. Gladstone was a British statesman, who was four times prime minister. A renowned orator, his policies were based on strong moral and religious convictions. He led a Liberal government, which achieved education, army and civil service reforms but in his last ministry was defeated over the Irish Home Rule Bill.

The Glassblower, Glasshouse Street W1, has recently put up a sign showing in silhouette a man blowing a glass vessel. The Soho area originally housed a large number of small craftsmen who made use of the houses and shops in the area. Glassblowers were amongst them.

Glasshouse Stores, Brewer Street W1. The sign depicts a craftsman working an orange blob of glass.

Globe Tavern, Bedale Street SE1. This pub was notorious for a fire in 1807 in which twenty lodgers were killed but the landlord and his family escaped. The name is linked to the nearby Globe Theatre built in 1588 reputedly with Shakespeare as one of the financiers of the building. The **Globe**, Bow Street WC2 (now closed), with a large globe positioned in front of it was a favourite pub for opera-goers as it was opposite to the Royal Opera House and therefore well patronised in the intervals. The original meaning of the sign could either indicate the spread of the British Empire across the world or in a narrower sense that the pub sold wines and port from Portugal. The **Globe Tavern**, Marylebone Road NW1 has three large signs depicting the world in three parts: North and South America, Europe and Africa, and Asia and Australia. The pub was built in 1735 when Marylebone Road was first laid out. It was patronised by William Pitt (prime minister 1783-1801, 1804-06), Charles Dickens and Sir Arthur Conan Doyle. This is one of the many London pubs with a resident ghost. In 1836 the landlord William Thornton lay ill or drunk in his bed. He asked his barmaid to collect some wine from the cellar. When she got back, she found him lying dead with his throat cut. The verdict given was suicide but William may not have agreed with this and his ghost is said to haunt the pub seeking justice.

Gloucester Arms, Gloucester Road SW7. The coat of arms etched on the windows, a royal coat of arms, edged with a blue and white bordure is that of a medieval Duke of Gloucester but the sign shows the arms of the city of Gloucester.

The Goat, Kensington High Street W8. A pub is reputed to have stood on this site for 300 years. In 1707 it was purchased by the vicar and churchwardens of St Mary Abbots for £80 and became a meeting place for parishioners. It was rebuilt in 1771 and altered in 1814 when it was used by local organisations such as the Kensington Paving Commissioners. In 1878 Watney and Co. of the Stag Brewery secured the lease and later bought the pub. The present building with its handsome sign of a goat dates from 1879. **Goat Tavern**, Stafford Street W1, housed in an eighteenth-century building, has the sign of a goat's head, and a golden model of a goat above the door.

The Golden Fleece, Queen Street EC4 has a large amount of art nouveau decoration. The sign depicts Jason holding the golden fleece. A golden fleece was also the badge of the Order of the

Left: *The Golden Fleece, Queen Street EC4*

Below: *The Golden Lion, Dean Street W1*

Golden Fleece founded in 1430 by Philip, Duke of Burgundy and sometimes bestowed upon Englishmen.

Golden Lion. This is the heraldic badge both of Henry II and of the Percy family, Dukes of Northumberland. The **Golden Lion**, Dean Street W1 has a splendid iron sign, sprayed gold. The **Golden Lion**, Fulham High Street SW6 has a golden lion rampant against a black background. The **Golden Lion**, King Street SW1 with its metallic sign is a continuation of a pub on this site since 1762. The architects Eedie and Meyers who created some of London's finest pubs from the 1880s until the Second World War built this particular pub. There is a wealth of decoration including carved lions and leaded windows, which continue the lion theme. It was next to the St James's Theatre, which was demolished in 1957, and many mementoes of the former theatre survive in the pub. There is even a theatre bar upstairs.

The Goldsmith's, Southwark Bridge Road, SE1 and the **Goldsmith's Arms**, Croydon Road SE25 both display coats of arms akin to those of the Worshipful Company of Goldsmiths. The company were the first bankers and were granted a charter in 1327.

Gracies, Elmers End Road SE20. This pub, originally called the **W.G. Grace**, had a sign commemorating the famous cricketer who lived in the area and captained the London County Cricket Club at Crystal Palace Park between 1899 and 1905.

The Grafton Arms, Grafton Way WC1. The sign shows Henry Fitzroy's coat of arms but with the bar sinister (or as heraldic terminology states 'debruised by the baton sinister') to indicate his royal descent but also his illegitimacy. (*See* the **Fitzroy Tavern**.)

Grand Union, Woodfield Street W9 is a recently renovated Victorian pub, which takes its name from the canal. The **Grand**

The Grafton Arms,
Grafton Way W1

Union, Camden Road NW1, although having no sign, also takes its name from the nearby Grand Union Canal.

Grapes. A very popular name for a pub. The name originally related to signs showing that the establishment sold wine rather than beer. Pubs of this name can be called the **Grapes** or the **Bunch of Grapes** and display an appropriate sign. The **Bunch of Grapes** in Brompton Road SW7 dates from 1777 when Henry Holland began building what he called Hans Town with houses for the upper and middle classes. By 1800 the development had stretched along what is now the Brompton Road and refreshment was needed for travellers. The pub was rebuilt in 1844 and has recently been refurbished. The **Bunch of Grapes**, St Thomas Street SE1 has one bunch but the tendrils are skillfully arranged to make eyes and a mouth. A similar sign is on the **Grapes**, Fairfield Street SW18 but as these two pubs belong to the same brewery, this is not surprising. This pub, built in 1833, was then licensed to sell only beer; it did not have a full licencee until 1849. The **Bunch of Grapes**, Lime Street EC3 has three ripe bunches with attendant vine leaves. The **Grapes**, Narrow Street E14, with its sign of two bunches of grapes, was built in 1720 replacing a pub, or its successor, on the site since the 1580s. There are ship's models and photos of local scenes on the walls. It is one of several pubs claiming to be 'The Six Jolly Fellowship Porters' in *Our Mutual Friend* (*See* the **Prospect of Whitby**). Dickens describes it as having, 'long settled into a state of hale infirmity. In its whole construction it had not a straight flow, and hardly a straight line'. In the 1970s the pub was given a major restoration but there is still a sense of unease as to the architecture as one enters. (*See* also **Ye Grapes**.)

Grave Maurice, Whitechapel Road E1. The sign shows Graaf Maurits, Prince of Orange, Count of Nassau (1567-1625), who helped to rid the Netherlands of their Spanish overlords.

Great Western, Praed Street W2. The pub, suitably placed near Paddington, the terminus of the Great Western Railway, still has signs depicting three steam locomotives for the GWR. Regrettably these have now faded and are difficult to decipher.

Green Man, Euston Road NW1 (which shows him holding a pint pot) and Riding House Street W1. The Green Man is a very ancient sign, which, although sometimes associated with Robin Hood, has nothing to do with this character but has its origins in pagan times, and is often known as Jack of the Green, He may be a fertility symbol and appears carved or painted in churches as an attempt to tame his powers. Green men often appear in pageants and were once part of the Lord Mayor's Show. Both the signs mentioned above depict him as the wild man covered with leaves and indicating his association with nature. The **Green Man**, Poultry EC2 shows the head of a man surrounded by leaves which grow from his mouth, which is a medieval concept. The sign of the

Green Man, Euston Road NW1

Green Man, Berwick Street W1 shows him as a wild man dressed in green leaves wielding a club; behind him figures dance round a maypole which refers to the fact that he was associated with May Day celebrations. The **Green Man**, Putney Heath SW15 dates from the eighteenth century and as usual was a haunt of highwaymen, including Dick Turpin. The highwayman, Jerry Abershaw, was hanged on a nearby gibbet in 1795. The sign depicts a woodman, possibly the head ranger, dressed in green clothing and hat with an axe over his shoulder.

Green Man and French Horn, St Martin's Lane WC2 has a sign, high up on the frontage, of a man dressed in green blowing a French horn.

The Greencoat Boy, Greencoat Place SW1. The Greencoat Hospital, which once stood in Tothill Fields, was founded by Charles I to help poor male orphans. The sign depicts a boy in the uniform of green coat and white trousers.

The Grenadier, Wilton Row SW1. This pub, tucked away in a side street, was originally an officers' mess for the Duke of Wellington's guards' regiments; military equipment lines the walls. Outside there is a sentry box and the mounting block said to have been used by the Duke of Wellington. The sign shows the head and shoulders of a soldier in grenadier's uniform. The ghost of a soldier killed for cheating at cards haunts the pub. (*See* colour picture 14.)

The Greyhound, Kirkdale SE26. This pub has the distinction of being the oldest one in the area being recorded in 1727. The sign showed a greyhound until it came under the auspices of the Firkin

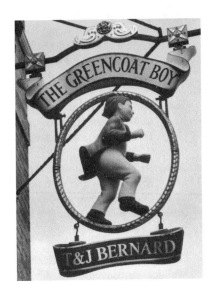

The Greencoat Boy, Greencoat Place SW1

Brewery and was renamed the **Firkin and Fewterer**. It has now reverted to the Greyhound and the sign depicts a greyhound in racing colour.

The Grosvenor Arms, Grosvenor Street W1, an early Victorian pub, is on land belonging to the Grosvenor Estate. The Grosvenor family fortunes began in 1677 when Sir Thomas Grosvenor married the heiress Mary Davis thereby gaining 300 acres of farmland in what became some of the richest parts of London, stretching through what is now Pimlico, Belgravia and Mayfair. The sign shows the early Grosvenor Arms without supporters but with the motto *Virtus non Stemma* (virtue not ancestry). (*See* the **Audley Arms**.)

The Guinea, Bruton Mews W1. A guinea, in pre-decimal coinage was £1 1s 0d and goods were often priced as this especially in shops selling superior goods. The pub, which stands on a site occupied by an alehouse from at least the seventeenth century and probably before that, was rebuilt entirely in the eighteenth century to cater for the servants, grooms and coachmen of the nearby large houses. It was once a mews alehouse and retains some of the atmosphere. It was known as the **Pound and Shilling** and is said to have antecedents as far back as the fifteenth century.

The Gun Inn, Coldharbour E14. This pub was once called the **King and Queen**, then the **Ramsgate Pink**. The name comes either from a gun foundry situated at Coldharbour or from the firing of Henry Addington's gun as his ship entered Blackwall Basin being the first ship into the newly-created dock area. It was rebuilt in the nineteenth century but the previous pub was reputed to be where Nelson met Emma Hamilton when he returned from his battles. This pub is certainly a naval pub having its wooden ceilings plastered with naval flags.

The Gunmakers, Aybrook Street W1 was formerly the **William Wallace** with a sign depicting the Scottish hero and the interior

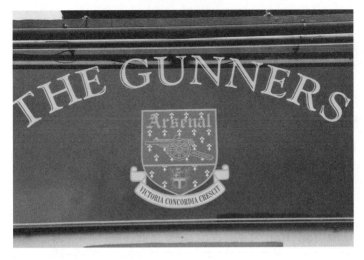

The Gunners, Blackstock Road N4

filled with stills from *Braveheart* and Scottish prints. After a total make over some prints remain – as do the bare floorboards but there is now a locked cabinet containing bullets and cartridges. The sign shows a gun maker, breaking his rifle.

The Gunners, Blackstock Road N4. The sign shows the badge of the Arsenal Football Club, which took its name from the fact that it was founded in 1886 at Woolwich Arsenal where guns and ammunition were manufactured. In 1913 the club leased the sports ground of St John's College of Divinity and moved to Highbury. From the pub Arsenal Stadium is visible but since 2006 the club has been relocated elsewhere and the former stadium is being converted to housing. The pub contains photographs of events relating to the history of 'the Gunners'.

H

The Half Moon, Lower Richmond Road SW15 has a sign depicting a smiling part of the moon.

Hamilton Hall, Liverpool Street Station EC2 is the former banqueting hall of the Great Eastern Hotel, which closed in 1939 and has recently been refurbished. The decoration is based on a room in the Palais Sorbise in Paris with a great deal of gilded stucco, cherubs, golden chandeliers, huge mirrors and paintings.

The Hand & Racquet, Whitcomb Street WC2 was founded as a brewery by Henry Whitcomb who gave his name to the street. The name is taken from a tennis court used by Charles II to play real tennis and the theme is continued with the walls decorated with tennis and badminton racquets. The pub was frequented by comedians such as Sid James and Tommy Cooper. Tony Hancock used this name in his radio comedies for his fictitious pub in East Cheam.

The Hand & Shears, Middle Street EC3. The pub stands on the site of a twelfth-century alehouse which served the monks and guests of St Bartholomew's Priory. The sign, which is the guild sign of the Merchant Tailors' Co., commemorates their role in the Smithfield Fair or St Bartholomew's Fair held at Michaelmas every September and one of the largest in London. The officials of the company checked the cloth to ensure that the cloth was sold with

*The Hand & Shears, Middle
Street EC3*

the right measure. The Lord Mayor opened the fair, first recorded in
1133, by cutting the first piece of cloth, which seems to have given
rise to the tradition of cutting a piece of tape to open an event. The
last Cloth Fair was held in 1855. The pub claims to have provided
refreshment to those who wished to watch the prisoners leave
Newgate Prison for their execution at Tyburn.

The Hare, Cambridge Heath Road W2 has a sign of a very perky
hare sitting up.

The Harringay Arms, Crouch Hill N8 dates back to the 1850s.
The name is taken from the district although this is now called
Harringey, the 'e' being a subtle inclusion of a vowel of Hornsey
when that district was merged with Harringay in the 1960s.

The Harrington, Gloucester Road SW7 dates from the 1880s and takes its name from Lord Harrington.

The Harrow, Whitefriars Street EC4 is a somewhat odd sign to find in London but this sign is a splendid one showing two shire horses pulling the harrow.

The Haverstock Arms, Haverstock Hill NW3 seems to have lost its sign but on the wall is a mural of a horse pulling a dray loaded with barrels.

Hen and Chickens, St Paul's Road N1. This is a magnificent Victorian pub occupying a corner site. The sign shows a hen and her chickens in silhouette but what is important is that this is a sixty-seater theatre pub (the seats came from Brighton Pier). In drinking slang terminology, a hen is a huge drinking vessel and the chicken a smaller one.

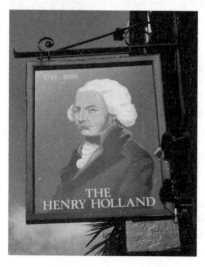

The Henry Holland, Duke Street W1

The Henry Holland, Duke Street W1. The pub sign commemorates the architect (1746-1806) who produced the first designs for the Brighton Pavilion, the Theatre Royal, Drury Lane, and the Royal Opera House. He laid out Sloane Square and several streets in Belgravia. The pub was rebuilt in 1956 on the site of a previous pub called the **Red Lion** and contains prints of Holland's architectural designs and his buildings.

Hereford Arms, Gloucester Road SW7. The sign shows the arms of Hereford. The pub claims to be one of the haunts of Jack the Ripper. If so, he was away from his haunts in the East End. One of the patrons was Sir Arthur Conan Doyle. During the Second World War the pub was patronised by American soldiers who had a baseball pitch in Hereford Square. The pub laments that the bill for broken windows was never paid.

Hercules Pillars, Great Queen Street WC2. (*See* **Pillars of Hercules**.)

Hero of Switzerland, Loughborough Road SW9. The sign depicts William Tell about to shoot the arrow to the apple on his son's head. Other signs show the Swiss flag and a Swiss chalet.

The Heron. This newly built pub in Norfolk Gardens W2 was originally the **Fountain** as it reflected the fountain, which was the central element in a block of flats built by the Church Commissioners. It now has an iron sign depicting a heron.

Hole in the Wall, Borough High Street SE1, is now called **The Trinity.** The name is applied to holes made by prisoners escaping from their cells, to spy holes and to breaches made in the walls of a town or castle. The latter appeared to be the case here.

Holly Bush, Holly Mount NW3. This pub was built on the site of a stable block in a house occupied by the artist George Romney

(1734-1802), who was one of the leading portrait painters of his time. He leased the stables to a victualling company who converted it into a tavern in the early 1800s.

Hoop & Grapes, Aldgate High Street EC3. The sign shows a bunch of grapes encircled by a hoop, which was a common sign for a public house, although this may originally have been Hop & Grapes alluding to beer and wine. Even so, the hoop encircled the barrel of beer and provided a framework for the vine. Originally built in 1598 and known by a different name, this pub is reputed to be the only pub which escaped the Great Fire of London. Parts of the building date from the late sixteenth century, with exposed brickwork and stone flags.

The Hoop & Toy, Thurloe Place SW7 once had a sign showing a child's hoop and rocking horse. Now without a sign the pub is still popular with visitors to the nearby museums.

Hoop & Grapes, Aldgate High Street W1

The Hop Pole, Putney Bridge Road SW18 shows a pole round which is trained a bind of hops. In the background are oast houses which are used for drying the hops to make beer. Many oast houses have now been converted to highly desirable residences. (*See* colour picture 15.)

The Hope, Tottenham Street W1 depicts the ship captured as a prize by Captain Mugford in 1776 and sailed to Boston. The **Hope**, Cowcross Street EC3 has a sign depicting two persons standing on a raft frantically waving to a ship on the horizon and hoping to be rescued, but the pub stands on the site of a former one which was founded at a time when Newgate Prison dominated the area. The 'hope' may come from the 'Path of Hope', taken by those condemned to execution. A variation on this theme is the **Hope and Anchor**, Crowndale Road NW1 (*See* the **Anchor and Hope**). The **Hope**, Norwood High Street SE27 has two hands releasing a dove, an obvious reference to the story of Noah's ark.

Horse & Groom, Great Portland Street W1. There are two signs painted on the façade. One depicts a brown horse patiently waiting to be harnessed; the other a groom resplendent in top hat, white breeches, red coat and highly polished boots. It is a reminder that behind many of the houses were mews where horses were stabled and carriages kept ready to convey the householders at a moment's notice. This also applied to the **Horse & Groom**, Groom Place SW1 tucked away in a small mews in Belgravia with a sign of a groom holding a horse.

Hung, Drawn and Quartered, Great Tower Street EC3, with its appropriate sign was once the administrative wing of Christ's Hospital, founded in 1552 and originally a charity school in London. The coat of arms of Christ's Hospital still remains above a door. Here prospective students and their parents were interviewed before being offered a free place for their education which later took place either at the girls' school at Hertford or the boys' school

Hung, Drawn and Quartered, Great Tower Street EC3

at Horsham. The girls' school has now closed and both girls and boys are educated at Horsham. Old prints inside the pub depict executions but a former pupil of the girls' school declared that the present name of the building aptly described her interview. The sign shows a prisoner being dragged before his executioner. On the wall is a quotation from Samuel Pepys' diary for 13 October 1660, 'I went to see Major General Harrison Hung, Drawn and Quartered. He was as cheerful as any man could be in that condition'.

I

Inn 1888, Devonshire Street W1. This is a peculiar name for a pub but relates to the fact that the building dates from 1888 and has been little altered. The sign, however, shows the arms of the Duke of Devonshire who held estates in the area in the seventeenth century.

The Intrepid Fox, Wardour Street W1. This does not refer to the wildlife of the area but to Charles James Fox (1749-1806), a Whig politician, who urged the abolition of slavery and toleration for

Inn 1888, Devonshire Street W1

The Intrepid Fox, Wardour Street W1

nonconformists. The 1784 election was a vicious fight between the Whigs and Tories in which the Tories emerged supreme. The landlord of the pub was one of Fox's greatest supporters. The sign immortalises Fox in stone as it shows the politician swaggering with his stick. The date 1784 recalls the election. Behind him is the innkeeper holding up a sign 'Champion of the People'.

The Iron Duke, Avery Row W1 has a portrait of the Duke of Wellington on its sign while the theme is continued inside as the walls are lined with portraits of the duke and his military activities. The **Iron Duke**, Vauxhall Bridge Road SW1 has a sign with a profile of the duke.

Island Queen, Noel Road N1. Although the sign displays a Mississippi river boat the name once referred to Queen Victoria who was devotedly attached to Osborne House on the Isle of Wight. She died there in 1901. The pub has embraced its maritime theme as the walls are covered with prints showing ships of a bygone era. There is also a wooden figurehead at the rear.

The Iron Duke, Avery Row W1

Island Queen, Noel Road N1

J

Jeremy Bentham, University Street WC1, the sign shows a portrait of the political economist (1748-1832) who was the spiritual founder of University College, the first college of London University. His skeleton, wearing his clothes and with a wax head is in the college. The embalmed head is kept in the college vaults. It is brought to meetings of the college council and is recorded as having been present but in a non-voting capacity. His philosophy of Utilitarianism was based on the concept that men's needs were dictated by pleasure and that the, 'state's concern is to give the greatest happiness to the greatest number'. The original name of the pub was the **Lord Wellington** but it was renamed in October 1982 to commemorate the 150th anniversary of Bentham's death.

The Jerusalem Tavern, Britton Street EC1, is a small building dating back to 1720, through having the sign of the head of St John on a platter, has reference to the Knights Templar who protected pilgrims on their way to and from the Holy Land. The Templars were suppressed in 1314 and their duties were taken over by the Knights Hospitallers, the Knights of St John of Jerusalem, whose priory was close by.

1 *The Artillery Arms, Bunhill Row EC1*

2 *The Australian, Milner Street SW3*

3 The Bricklayers Arms, Dartmouth Road SE26

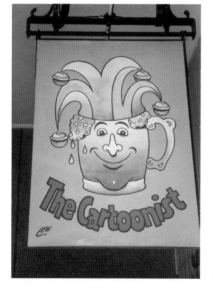

4 The Cartoonist, Shoe Lane EC4

5 *The Colonies, Wilfred Street SW1*

6 *Coopers Arms, Flood Street SW1*

7 *The Crutched Friar, Crutched Friars EC3*

8 *Dirty Dicks, Bishopsgate EC2*

9 The Duke, Wells Road SE26

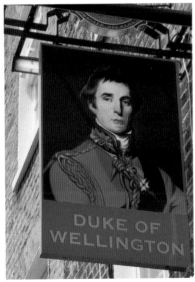

*10 Duke of Wellington, Eaton Terrace
SW1*

11 *Emma Hamilton, Kingston Road SW20*

12 *The Fitzroy Tavern, Charlotte Street W1*

13 *The George, Borough High Street SE1*

14 *The Grenadier, Wilton Row SW1*

15 The Hop Pole, Putney Bridge Road SW18

16 Kings Arms, Newcomen Street SE1

17 *King's Arms, Wandsworth High Street SW18*

18 *Mabel's Tavern, Mabledon Place WC1*

19 *The Mudlark, Montague Close SE1*

20 *The Old Dr. Butler's Head, Masons Avenue EC2*

21 Phene Arms, Phene Street SW3

22 The Prospect of Whitby,
Wapping Way E1

23 Punch & Judy, Covent Garden WC2

24 The Queens Larder, Queen Street WC1

25 The Rose & Crown, Wandsworth High Street SW18

26 The Rugby Tavern, Great James Street WC1

Above: *27 Sir Alexander Fleming,
St Michael's Street W1*

Left: *28 The Swan Tavern, Ship
Tavern Passage EC*

29 The Victoria, Strathearn Place W2

30 The Wheatsheaf, Stoney Street SE1

Left: *31 The White Hart, Giltspur Street EC1*

Below: *32 Yorkshire Grey, Langham Street W1*

John Snow, Broadwick Street W1. The pub, originally called the **Newcastle-upon-Tyne**, since 1955 quite rightly has a sign depicting John Snow (1813-58), a London doctor of obstetrics, anaesthesia and epidemiology. During a cholera outbreak in London in 1854, he analysed the geography of the water supply and the mortality patterns in this area of Soho. He noted that the largest number of cases came in the vicinity of a single water pump on Broad Street. This pump drew its water from the heavily contaminated well. Snow reasoned that cholera conveyed by water was the cause of so many deaths and insisted that the pump handle was removed. Although the pump was soon back in use Snow's work was recognised as one of the great discoveries in public health. The pub, which dates from the early eighteenth century, was renamed in the 1950s to commemorate Snow and has a John Snow room giving details of his work and a plaque on the outside wall

The Jerusalem Tavern, Britton Street EC1

Jeremy Bentham, University Street WC1

John Snow, Broadwick Street W1   *The Jolly Gardeners, Black Prince Road W1*

notes the site of the pump. The pub was also the local of William Blake (1757-1827), the poet and visionary who lived in nearby Poland Street, where he wrote his poems published under the title *Songs of Innocence*.

Jolly Gardeners, Lower Richmond Road SW14 has a sign depicting three men having a drink. On closer inspection one is a scarecrow. **The Jolly Gardeners**, Black Prince Road SE1 has two signs. One is placed in stucco above the door and would take some moving. This displays two swaggering men, one with spade, and the other with a scythe. The other sign has two jolly gardeners with one leaping for joy that the other has dug up a carrot.

The Jolly Sailor, High Street SE25, with its happy sign, is a nineteenth-century pub, which gave its name to a station of the London & Croydon Co. Line. In 1845 the station became Norwood Junction, named after the district.

K

Kembles Head, Long Acre WC2 has now a sign replacing a former one, each reputing to portray the actor Philip Kemble, said to be the finest actor of his time and the first of a long line of actor managers. He took over the Covent Garden Theatre in 1803.

The King & Keys, Fleet Street EC4 has a sign showing crossed keys and a crown.

King and Queen, Foley Street W1. The sign depicts a silhouette of the King leaning forward to kiss the Queen's hand.

The King's Arms. A very popular sign as formerly it often demonstrated loyalty to the monarchy. Some signs display the head of a king as does the **King's Arms** in Chiswell Street EC1 that portrays George II (1727-60). Others have the royal coat of arms with lion and unicorn as supporters. Good ones are to be seen in King William Walk SE10, Shepherd Market W1 and Newcomen Street SE1. The last has three identical signs, one in stone. This was removed from London Bridge when it was taken down in 1780 and the material was sold by auction. The stone coat of arms displays the arms of the monarchy in the time of George III (1760-1820). Above the arms is the inscription 'GEO III' and the date 1760. The **King's Arms**, Poland Street W1 displays the arms of England and France quartered within an oval shape surrounded by the garter with the garter motto. The supporters are a lion and a dragon. The Ancient Order of Druids was revived here in 1787. The **King's Arms**, Wandsworth High Street SW18 has a splendid punning sign depicting the torso of a man dressed in a leather doublet and white-sleeved shirt. No head is visible but there appear to be locks of hair draped over the jerkin. (*See* colour pictures 16 and 17.)

The King's Head, Upper Street N1 displays a head of George IV (1820-30). This is the oldest theatre pub in London, having had live performances of great variety since the 1970s. The **King's Head**, Westmoreland Street W1 is another theatre pub, which displays the head of Henry VIII on its sign. Inside there is a list of landlords since 1841 but the pub dates back to 1732 when one of its employees was Charlotte Cibber, daughter of Colly Cibber, poet laureate to George II. She disguised herself as a man so that she could wait on the clientele, not a difficult task for her as she had acted in the London theatres. The **King's Head**, High Street SW15, with its sign of a doleful Charles I should be mentioned although the future of the pub is uncertain even though it is a listed building. It was originally known as the **Bull** and is reputed to date from the fifteenth century, but was known by its present name in the seventeenth century. The **King's Head**, Stratton Street W1 displays the head of George II and to emphasis this has the initials 'G II' at the top of the sign. The **King's Head**, Upper Tooting Road, SW17 is a massive Victorian pub, built in 1896, which still retains the best work of the craftsmen of the time, especially the embossed glass.

The Kings Head and Eight Bells, Chelsea SW3, which has a sign depicting Charles II surrounded by eight bells, may have obtained its name from the amalgamation of two pubs or because bells were rung as the King was rowed past on the Thames.

King William IV, Hampstead High Street NW3. The sign shows the arms of William IV. (*See* **William IV**.)

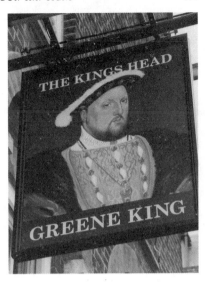

The Kings Head, Westmoreland Street W1

The Knights Templar, Chancery Lane WC2 has no sign but deserves to be mentioned for its name. The Knights Templar was founded in Jerusalem in 1118 to protect pilgrims who were going to visit the Holy Sepulchre. Its members were soldiers and monks vowed to poverty, chastity and obedience. When the Holy Land was lost after the Fall of Acre in 1291 the order lost its purpose and its wealth aroused the jealousy of Philip IV of France. In 1307 he forced Pope Clement V to condemn the order, arrested all the Templars in France and tried them for heresy and treason. The order was abolished in 1314 and their wealth and lands confiscated. In England the knights were allowed to disperse but their lands were confiscated, many of them being handed over to the Knights Hospitallers. They leased some of the London land to Professors of Common Law, who together with their students, gathered in the area south of Fleet Street. It is this area which forms the Middle Temple and the Inner Temple, now two of the Inns of Court.

L

The Lamb, Lamb's Conduit Street WC1. The pub, which has a sign of a small lamb, is named after William Lamb, a member of the Clothworkers' Co. who improved a water conduit in 1577 and gave pails to the poor so that they could obtain water. Sir Christopher Wren later redesigned the conduit. The original building dates from the 1720s but has been refurbished several times, the last in the 1960s although the Victorian interior has been kept. On the walls are portraits of Victorian music hall stars. The **Lamb Tavern**, Leadenhall Market EC3, which unfortunately has no sign, dates from 1780. It contains tiled pictures of the Great Fire of London (1666) and of Sir Christopher Wren with his plans for the monument which commemorates that fire.

Lamb and Flag, Rose Street WC2. After the Reformation it became a sign of a flag resting against a lamb, a lamb with a banner wrapped round it or a lamb holding a cross. It originally identified St John the Baptist and as such can been seen on paintings identifying the saint and referring to the verse in *St John's Gospel* (1:29), 'behold the lamb of God which taketh away the sin of the world'. A pictorial sign was adopted as the heraldic device of the Knights Templar and the Merchant Tailors' Co. The Rose Street pub was once known as the **Coopers' Arms** relating to the company, which provided the barrels for the beer and also as the **Bucket of Blood** because of the bare fisted-fights which took place there.

The sign of the **Lamb and Flag**, James Street W1 displays a lamb draped with the Union Flag.

The Lambeth Walk, Lambeth Road SE1. The sign shows a 'toff' in top hat and tails swaying to the *Lambeth Walk* which was a line dance, originally devised for the musical, *Me and My Gal*, in 1937 by a then popular comedian, Lupino Lane. This soon became extremely popular. The words began:

> Any evening, any day,
> Once you go down Lambeth Way,
> You'll find them all, doing the Lambeth walk, Oy.

The Leather Bottle, Kingston Road SW20 displays a sign showing a man swigging from a leather bottle, the usual container before glass bottles became the norm, which could be carried when away from home and was always available for a handy drink. The **Leather Bottle**, Garret Lane SW17 dates from the eighteenth century.

Leinster Arms, Leinster Terrace W2 displays the arms of the Duke of Leinster, *argent a saltire gules* with supporters of two monkeys enchained.

The Lemon Tree, Bedfordbury WC1. The sign shows a lemon tree with a man and a dog under it. The name may refer to the former fruit and vegetable market at Covent Garden. The pub is now the local of English National Opera, whose stage door is next to it.

The Lion & Lamb, Fanshaw Street N1 has a sign of a lion rampant, facing a lamb also rampant but with a stick and a swag bag over its shoulder as if it is meaning to depart to distant fields.

Lion & Unicorn, Gainsford Street NW5. These supporters of arms rear up on the sign. This is one of north London's theatre inns. The lion and the unicorn were adopted as heraldic supporters by

James I. Unicorns are mythical beasts with the body of a horse, the tail of a lion and a single horn protruding from the forehead. They became immortalised in the children's nursery rhymes.

Lord Aberconway, Old Broad Street EC2. The man whom the pub commemorates was the last chairman of the Metropolitan Railway. The pub was formerly named the **King and Keys** and claims that the refreshment room and railway buffet are haunted by people who died in the Great Fire of 1666.

The Lord Burghley, Vauxhall Bridge Road SW1. The pub sign depicts William Cecil (1520-98), created Baron Burghley in 1571 as well as being the trusted advisor to Elizabeth I.

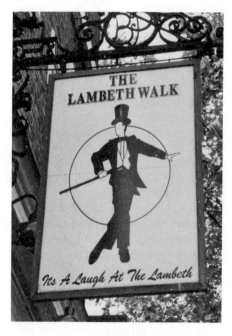

The Lambeth Walk,
Lambeth Road SE1

The Lord Clyde, Glenman Street SE1. The sign depicts a portrait of Lord Clyde (1792-1863). Originally Sir Colin Campbell he was a distinguished soldier whose career began in the Peninsular War. He served in China, was Lieutenant Governor of Canada, commanded the Highland Brigade in the Crimea and played a major part in the victory gained at the battle of Balaclava (1854). He was Commander-in-Chief of the British Army in India at the time of the Indian Mutiny and gained fame for relieving the Siege of Lucknow (1857). He was created Baron Clyde the following year. A landlord of the pub had served under the Field Marshall and named the pub after him.

Lord John Russell, Marchmont Street WC1. The sign depicts the statesman, first Earl Russell (1792-1878), better known as Lord John Russell, who was twice prime minister (1846-52, 1865-66). As foreign secretary in 1862 he kept Britain from intervening in the American Civil War.

The Lord Moon of the Mall, Whitehall SW1. The name and sign are a twentieth-century invention but the interior is one of solid splendour. It was originally a banking headquarters of Cocks, Biddulph & Co., later Barclays Bank built in 1872 and refurbished in 1902. There are vaulted ceilings, marbled walls, paintings, shelves of library books, and other decorations. The feeling is that of a gentleman's club.

The Lord Nelson, Union Street SE1 is a nondescript estate pub but the sign is a splendid portrait of the admiral. Horatio Nelson, first Viscount Nelson, (1758-1805), born in Burnham Thorpe, Norfolk was perhaps England's greatest naval hero. His death at the Battle of Trafalgar (1805), when he destroyed the combined French and Spanish fleets, resulted in national mourning. The **Nelson Arms**, Merton High Street SW20 has a portrait of the admiral. **Nelson's Retreat**, Vince Street EC1 shows Lord Nelson relaxing in his cabin.

*The Lord Clyde, Glenmar Street
SE1*

*Lord John Russell, Marchmont
Street WC1*

The Lord Palmerston, Childers Street SE8. Henry John, Viscount Palmerston (1784-65,) was a statesman who was twice prime minister. Previously as foreign secretary he had secured Belgium independence in 1830; later he was to support Italian nationalism.

Lord Raglan, St Martin-le-Grand EC4. Fitzroy James Henry Somerset, first Baron Raglan (1788-1855) was Commander-in-Chief of the British forces during the Crimean War. He is regrettably remembered mainly for his part in the destruction of the Light Brigade so vividly portrayed in the poem by Tennyson. The pub, formerly called the **Bush**, is said to be situated on one of the oldest pub sites in the City. The cellars contain parts of the original Roman wall.

Lord Rodney's Head, Whitechapel Road E1 displays a portrait of George Brydges, Admiral Lord Rodney (1718-92). He distinguished himself by defeating a French and Spanish fleet at the 'Battle of the Saintes' in 1782 in the Caribbean, which secured the island of Jamaica for the British Crown.

The Lord Stanley, Camden Park Road NW1. The sign depicts the bust of a Tudor nobleman. The Stanleys came in on Henry Tudor's side at the Battle of Bosworth Field (August 1485) thus ensuring Henry's victory over Richard III. Lord Stanley placed the battered crown of England on the head of Henry. For this support and to mark Henry's official Coronation on 30 October 1485, Thomas, Lord Stanley was created first Earl of Derby.

The Lord Wolseley, White Lion Street N1 has a sign showing Sir Garnet Wolseley (1833-1913), later Field Marshall, the first Viscount Wolseley, in full dress uniform with his Field Marshall's baton. He served in India taking part in the Relief of Lucknow, in China and in Canada. He became Commander-in-Chief of the British army in 1895. His main achievements were to secure the Gold Coast for

Lyceum Tavern, Strand WC2

the British Crown in 1874 and to ensure the British occupation of Egypt by his victory at Tel-el-Kabir in 1882.

Lyceum Tavern, Strand WC2. The pub takes its name from the nearby Lyceum Ballroom, which has now become a theatre. A sign (now removed) depicted an actor, probably Sir Henry Irving, putting on his make-up.

M

Mabel's Tavern, Mabledon Place WC1. A punning sign based on the location. The barmaid in mop cap holds tankards on a tray. (*See* colour picture 18.)

The Macbeth, Hoxton Street N1 was originally Hoxton's Distillery. There was once a splendid sign of Macbeth, in highland garb with claymore, but this has now gone. One hopes that this is not a consequence of the bad luck attached to the play's name.

The Magdala, South Hill Park NW3. The name refers to the battle in 1868 in which Sir Robert Napier stormed the then capital of Ethiopia. The pub is notorious for being the site where Ruth Ellis shot her lover as he came out of the pub. She was the last woman to be hanged in England.

The Magog, Russia Row EC2 has now been lost forever. Gog and Magog were symbols of the world's hostility to the church but as far as London was concerned they were gatekeepers of the city and part of the legendry history of London. Two figures once guarded the entrance to the pub.

Magpie and Stump, Old Bailey EC4. Although the pub set within a modern building development of the 1990s is but a shadow of its former self it is still in the inheritor of a great tradition. It is the successor of several pubs which have stood on this site and been patronised by those on both sides of the law, the criminals and the lawyers. In its glory days it was known as Court Number Ten where legal arguments could be hammered out. Lunch was often sent across to the prisoners on trial at the Old Bailey across the way. When Newgate Prison stood opposite, the pub's windows provided a grandstand view for the hangings, which took place in front of the jail. At one time it was called the **King of Denmark** when James I married Anne of Denmark and then the **Dutch Kitchen** after the manner of cooking by Dutch ovens. These were roasting tins with a movable cowl to direct the heat of an open fire onto the meat.

Maple Leaf, Maiden Lane WC2. This pub, once the **Bedford Head**, is now a Canadian theme pub with its back premises resembling a log cabin, a framed mounties' uniform and a moose head. The front has signs depicting a maple leaf.

The Market Porter, Stoney Street SE1 has an appropriate sign showing a porter bowed under the weight of a basket on his head and a basket in his hand. The pub is appropriately situated as it once served porters at the nearby Borough Market. Within the last ten years the market has now become a market supplying high-class product on a retail basis to a variety of customers.

The Marlborough Arms, Torrington Place WC1 has a sign representing the arms of the Dukes of Marlborough. The first duke, John Churchill (1650-1722) was a brilliant soldier who led the English army during the Seven Years' War, in which his greatest victory was the Battle of Blenheim in 1704. For this his grateful sovereign Queen Anne presented him with Blenheim Palace.

The Marlborough Head, North Audley Street W1. The pub is part of the Eerie Chain Pub Co. chain but there are three handsome signs of the duke wearing a full-bottomed wig and looking disdainfully down on the clientele.

The Market Porter, Stoney Street SE1

The Marlborough Head, North Audley Street W1

Marquis of Anglesey, Bow Street WC2. The pub stands on the site of a victualling premises and of the Edward Miles Coffee house both known in the seventeenth century. It has a splendid sign depicting a portrait of Henry William Paget, first Marquis of Anglesey (1768-1854) who was commander of the cavalry at the Battle of Waterloo in 1815. During the battle a cannon ball shot off his right leg. 'By God, Sir', he said to the Duke of Wellington, 'I think I have lost my leg'. 'By God, Sir', replied the Duke, 'So you have'. The leg was preserved in Powys Castle and buried with the Marquis when he died forty years later. (*See* the **Anglesey Arms**.)

Marquis of Granby. The Marquis is usually depicted by a half bust as in the signs in New Cross Road SE14, Dean Bradley Street SW1 and Rathbone Street WC1. John Manners, Marquis of Granby (1721-70), son of the third Duke of Rutland, was Colonel of the Royal Regiment of Horse Guards in 1758 and became Commander-in-Chief of the army in 1760. He was noted for his courage in battle often riding at the head of his troops as he did at the Battle of Warburg against the French during the Seven Years' War. During one charge his wig blew off and his bald head, shining in the sun, was said to have formed a 'guiding light' for his men giving rise to the saying 'going bald-headed for it'. He was extremely popular because he provided funds for disabled senior non-commissioned officers to set themselves up as tavern keepers when they had to leave the army at a time when no other funds were given to them. It was thus inevitable that they would name their pubs in honour of their patron. The **Marquis of Granby**, Chandos Place WC2 was once the **Hole in the Wall**. The highwayman Claude Duval was arrested here and was hanged at Tyburn in 1670.

Marquis of Westminster, Belgrave Road SW1. Robert Grosvenor, second Earl Grosvenor (1767-1845) was created first Marquis of Westminster in 1831. The sign depicts the Marquis in black frock coat, blue waistcoat and white cravat. (*See* the **Grosvenor Arms**.)

Marquis of Granby, Dean Bradley Street SW1

Marquis of Westminster, Belgrave Road SW1

Mason's Arms, Upper Berkeley Street W1. The cellars of the pub once housed condemned prisoners who were to be executed at Tyburn until the execution site was abandoned in 1783. The manacles are still on the walls.

The Mayflower, Rotherhithe Street SE16. This pub only became the Mayflower in 1957. The sign depicts what may have been the *Mayflower*, the historic ship that took the Pilgrim Fathers across the Atlantic. The building, originally called the **Shyppe**, has been restored but recalls the time when Captain Christopher Jones moored here before sailing in 1620 to Southampton to join with the *Speedwell* for their historic voyage across the Atlantic, and thence to Plymouth. The ships set sail on 6 September and arrived off the coast of New England on 21 December. Jones is buried in the parish church. Needless to say the pub is popular with Americans. A post office was established in the inn to serve sailors and watermen from the boats on the river. It still has the unique distinction of being able to sell English and American stamps from the bar.

The Mitre, Craven Terrace W2 is a classic Victorian pub with the sign of a mitre resting on a cushion.

Molly Moggs, Old Compton Street W1 is a theme pub displaying a sign with a barmaid wearing a mop cap holding a tray with a mug and a bottle of beer.

The Monarch, Cropley Street N1. A modern, undistinguished pub with a sign showing the head of Charles II.

The Monkey Puzzle. The pub in Sussex Gardens W2 takes its name from the monkey puzzle tree or Chilean pine that stands by the entrance. Its sign depicts the tree and the monkey.

The Morpeth Arms, Millbank SW1 stands on a busy corner by Vauxhall Bridge. Built in 1845 by Paul Dangerfield, the pub still

Left: *The Mitre, Craven Terrace W2*

Below: *The Monkey Puzzle, Sussex Gardens W2*

retains many original features, together with photographs of the area and information about the Millbank Penitentiary, which was built in 1813. This was not intended to be a prison but a place where criminals could be reformed. It soon became a holding prison in which prisoners were held before being transported to Australia. It was demolished in 1900 and the Tate Britain now occupies the site. The arms on the pub are those of Lord Morpeth, who was one of the chief commissioners for the improvement of London and responsible for developing this area. The pub has a resident ghost said to be a would-be escapee from the Millbank Penitentiary who wanders the labyrinthine passages beneath the pub.

The Mudlark, Montague Close SE1. This pub is situated underneath London Bridge. Appropriately the sign depicts two children, scavengers nicknamed mudlarks, sitting on the exposed foreshore at low tide across from the Houses of Parliament searching for anything that had saleable value. (*See* colour picture 19.)

The Mulberry Bush, Upper Ground SE1. This new pub displays a sign showing the old rhyme, *Here we go round the mulberry bush*. Theatre goers and concertgoers on the South Bank site patronise it.

Museum Tavern, Great Russell Street, WC1. A glance opposite will show the origin of this name, as the pub stands opposite the British Museum. The earliest record of an inn on this site dates to 1723 when it was called the **Dog and Duck** either because hunting for wild fowl took place in what were then fields or for the cruel sport of chasing a pinioned duck with dogs round a pond. The British Museum was founded in 1759 and the pub is known to have been called the **Museum Tavern**, when it was rebuilt about 1855. A previous sign depicted two ancient Egyptians drinking but the present one shows the head of Sir Hans Sloan, one of the founders of the museum, placed in front of the museum.

N

The Nags Head, James Street, WC2 and Kinnerton Street SW1. The signs depict the head of a white horse. The Covent Garden pub was originally a hotel serving patrons of the Royal Opera House and as such, opera bills and other memorabilia of opera decorate its walls. It is still a watering hole for artists and members of the opera house, especially the orchestra, who make excellent use of it during the intervals. The Kinnerton Street pub is unusual in that the staff stand on a lower floor than the bar. The pub displays caricatures of actors.

Nell Gwynne Tavern, Bull Inn Court WC1 in a narrow alleyway from the Strand, has a portrait of the actress who though only the mistress of Charles was reputed to have persuaded him to found the Royal Hospital, Chelsea. The pub, rebuilt in 1897, is said to be haunted by the ghost of the actor William Ferris who was killed in the alley outside the pub.

Nell of Old Drury, Catherine Street WC2. Nell Gwyn, the mistress of King Charles II, said to have been born in a house in Drury Lane, was originally an orange seller in Covent Garden market. The inn was reputed to have been first built about 1600 when the first Theatre Royal was built and to have had a secret passage between the inn and the theatre to enable Charles II to visit Nell Gwyn. The pub sign has an imaginative somewhat alluring visage of the actress/mistress. A previous sign showed a demure lady with a basket of oranges.

*The Nags Head, James Street
WC2*

Nellie Dean, Dean Street W1. The sign shows the head and shoulders of a woman wearing a black and purple dress and a black hat with purple trimmings. Nellie Dean, although a popular British song in the Victorian era and related to a fictitious character, was composed by an American, Henry W. Armstrong. It retained its popularity until the Second World War and was often sung in a drunken fashion.

The Nelson Arms. (*See* **Lord Nelson**.)

Nelson's Retreat. (*See* **Lord Nelson**.)

The New Market, Smithfield Street EC1. This pub was originally the **Market Porter**. The sign now depicts a porter pulling a barrow laden with meat. Behind him is one of the distinctive towers of Smithfield Market.

The New Market, Smithfield Street EC1

New Moon, Leadenhall Market EC3. A pub has stood on this site since the early eighteenth century. The present sign depicts a new moon above Tower Bridge.

The North Star, Finchley Road NW3 was built in 1850 as one of the first buildings on the new Finchley Road, which was an alternative to the old road out of London. This considerably eased the congestion. The stars on the top of the main pillar supports indicate the name but the main sign shows a polar bear hanging on to a star.

The Northumberland Arms, Tottenham Court Road W1 displays a shield with the colours of the Percys, Dukes of Northumberland. The **Northumberland Arms** Goodge Street W1 shows the full coat of arms picked out in gold against a blue background.

O

Old Bank of England, Fleet Street EC4. Built in 1888 at the suggestion of the Treasury, this was the former Law Courts branch of the Bank of England and it displays its origin with the elaborate murals, a huge carved bar, gilt chandeliers and dignified pillars. The former manager's office is now a club room. The bullion room, with steel-reinforced walls is now the wine and beer cellar, probably the safest one in the British Isles. The building was converted into a pub in 1995. It stands on the site of two former pubs, the **Cock**, now removed to the other side of Fleet Street and the **Haunch of Venison** supposed to have been the local pub of Sweeney Todd.

The Old Bell, Fleet Street EC4 was built in 1670 for the workmen and craftsmen rebuilding St Paul's Cathedral, who also worked on St Bride's church. Later, when Fleet Street was the place of the printing industry, it was a haunt of printers and newspapermen until gradually the industry moved to Canary Wharf over the 1970s and 1980s. Printers gathered here because this was the site where William Caxton set up the first printing press in England in the 1400s. When he died in 1491 Winkyn de Worde, his assistant, took over. Other printers gathered round him so that eventually Wynkyn was entitled the 'father of Fleet Street printing'. The **Old Bell**, Kilburn High Road NW6 was originally an eighteenth-century tea garden where people came to take the waters of Kilburn Wells. This was demolished and the present pub dates from 1863. It is one

*The Old Bell, Fleet Street
EC4*

of the many Irish pubs in this district that is referred to as County
Kilburn.

Old Blade Bone, Bethnal Green Road E1. The name comes from
the fact that there was a murder at the inn and the body was buried
in quicklime. When it was discovered the police took all the remains
away except for the shoulder blade which the landlord exhibited in
his pub.

The Old Bull and Bush, North End Way NW3, with its sign
depicting the name, may have obtained the name from a bull and
bushes or yew trees. This is the inn mentioned in the music hall
song *Down at the Old Bull and Bush*, a song made famous by the
Victorian singer Florrie Ford. It is based on a German tune and
was reputedly written in the garden at the inn. The pub began

as a country farmhouse about 1645 and gained its first license in
1721. Eminent persons said to have drunk here included Joshua
Reynolds, David Garrick and Thomas Gainsborough. Henry
Humphries became the landlord in 1867, obtained a music license
for musical entertainment and the song, once sung, was perpetuated.
The outside was modernised in 1924 and the interior reduced to
minimal decoration fairly recently.

> Do, do, come and have a drink or two
> Down at the old Bull and Bush,
> Bush, Bush.

The Old City Arms, Hammersmith Bridge Road W6 has photos
and prints of the river round Hammersmith Bridge. The sign is
a splendid one of the City of London Arms with supporters and
crest.

Old Coffee House, Beak Street W1. The sign depicts a group of
men sitting round a table being served by a woman bearing mugs of
beer or coffee. Coffee houses were very popular in the seventeenth
century when this new drink was introduced to London society.
Gradually alcoholic drinks intruded into the establishments.

Old Dispensary, Leman Street E1. This is a converted Victorian
medicine dispensary which once served the East End poor. It retains
the bare floorboards and its large high room with a gallery.

The Old Doctor Butler's Head, Masons Avenue EC2 dates back
to the seventeenth century and the approach down an original
alleyway perpetuates the illusion. Dr Butler was court physician to
James I, and practised a series of eccentric cures, such as dropping
people into the Thames from London Bridge. On the side he
developed an ale which was sold in taverns built to his instructions.
This one has survived. (*See* colour picture 20.)

The Old English Gentleman, Edgware Road W2 has a sign with a portly top-hatted figure with cane under arm surveying the scene.

Old King's Head, King's Head Yard, SE1 is down a side alley off Borough High Street. Many pubs with this name were originally named the Pope's Head but swiftly changed the name at the Reformation. It was rebuilt on the same site in 1881. The sign depicting Henry VIII on Borough High Street lures passers-by to the pub but there is a splendid bust of the King high on the façade.

Old Nick, Sandforth Street WC1. This is a splendid sign showing a dignified man dressed in what appears to be Renaissance garb. Nick is not the Devil but a friend of the owners of this pub's brewer company who gave large sums to charity and who is commemorated here. There are a number of prints of old London on the wall and the pub is frequented by members of Gray's Inn, the entrance to which is at the end of the street.

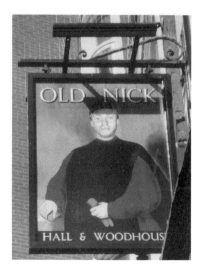

Old Nick, Sandforth Street E2

Old Nun's Head, Nunhead Green SE15. The sign displays a veiled nun. The future of this pub is uncertain but it was known to have been first licensed in the sixteenth century. It was built on the site of a nunnery suppressed during the Dissolution of the Monasteries in the 1530s. Most of the tales associated with it, for example that the mother superior was beheaded, are apocryphal.

The Old Red Lion, High Holborn WC1 displays a red lion rampant. The **Old Red Lion,** St John Street, EC1, begun in 1979, is another of London's theatre pubs, but it stands on the site of one opened in 1415. (*See* the **Red Lion**.)

The Old Swan, Kensington Church Street W8 once stood on the Roman road leading to the west. There has been a public house on the site for almost four hundred years and it was refurbished in the nineteenth century when the Great Western Railway Co. opened up the area.

Old Thameside Inn, Clink Street SE1. This pub, originally a spice warehouse, is situated by the side of the dock where there is a replica of the *Golden Hind*, the ship in which Sir Francis Drake (1540-96) circumnavigated the globe during 1577-80, for which he was knighted.

The One Tun, Goodge Street WC1 has the sign of a man lifting a barrel high into the air.

The Opera Tavern, Catherine Street WC2. This late nineteenth-century pub was originally called the **Sheridan Knowles** after an Irish playwright, whose first successful play was performed in Covent Garden in 1820. The name was changed to the **Opera Tavern** when George Treacher rebuilt it. The sign portrays an excellent reproduction of the façade of the Royal Opera House in nearby Bow Street and the inside has plenty of opera memorabilia.

The Owl & The Pussycat,
Redchurch Street E2

The Owl & The Pussycat, Redchurch Street, E2. The sign conveys exactly the poem created by Edward Lear (1812-88). The owl and the cat are in the boat with pots of honey and bags of money although the owl seems somewhat startled about their predicament.

The Oxford Arms, Camden High Street NW1. This Victorian pub is the home of the tiny Etcetera Theatre with its six rows of seats, which is reached from the rear of the bar. The sign displays the arms of the city of Oxford.

The Oxford & Cambridge, Hammersmith Bridge Road W6. This mock half-timbered pub has a sign depicting the arms of both universities and suggests a connection with either the universities or the boat race. Neither is the case, but a short walk to the river will give a view of the race.

P

The Packhorse and Talbot, Chiswick High Road W4 is a somewhat bland pub but has an interesting sign in the round of a packhorse preceded by a dog. The Talbot was a large dog often used as a guard dog. Packhorse owners would use it when they left their horses while seeking refreshment.

The Paradise, Kilburn Lane W10. Lines from G.K. Chesterton's poem, *To Paradise by Way of Kensal Green* are painted on the front of the bar counter in this old Victorian pub. A free-standing angel stands guard in a corner and the sign depicts an angel over a glass of wine.

The Paxton, Paxton Place SE27. Although this pub has been drastically altered and is now under another name, the previous sign showed the head of Sir Joseph Paxton and the name obviously commemorated the man who brought fame to the local area.

The Paxton's Head, Knightsbridge SW1 is a traditional Victorian pub, which commemorates the fact that Sir Joseph Paxton (1803-65), whose head is displayed on the sign, designed the Crystal Palace in 1851 for the Great Exhibition in Hyde Park. When the exhibition had closed the glass palace was to be demolished but Paxton organised its transference to Sydenham, South London. The palace and pleasure park were so great that they gave the name

Crystal Palace to the district in south London. The pub was the
watering hole for the men who built the Great Exhibition glass
palace. The name comes from a remark made by a prime minister
that 'Paxton's Head has been turned' meaning that 'he was getting
above himself'.

The Pembroke Castle, Gloucester Avenue NW1. The sign is the
Pembroke Arms. (*See* the **Dublin Castle**.)

The Pepper Pot, Dock Street E1. The sign depicts a man sitting by
sacks of pepper. In front of him are a pepper grinder and a pepper
pot. From a basket, black pepper corns spill out. The pub is near
to the docks where spices were unloaded until the Second World
War.

The Perseverance, Pritchard's Road E2. This modern pub now
has no sign but previously it had one displaying a mountaineer, with
snow goggles and pickaxe, climbing a mountain.

Phene Arms, Phene Street SW3. The pub is named after a local
worthy, Dr John Phene whose mission was to plant trees throughout
London. In this work he had encouragement from Queen Victoria.
The inn displays the Phene coat of arms. (*See* colour picture 21.)

The Phoenix, Cavendish Square W1. The phoenix was a
mythological bird which when it felt the onset of death set fire to
itself and was reborn from the ashes. It may be used heraldically as
referring to the Dukes of Somerset. This modern pub sign depicts
the bird in black silhouette against a yellow background. The
Phoenix, Alexandra Palace N22 has a more interesting sign showing
the bird sitting on the flames, which will devour it. This pub, which
is integral to the palace, was originally the **Panorama** because of
the spectacular view over north-east London. It was refurbished in
the 1970s in what purports to be the 1930s Art Deco style.

The Phoenix, Cavendish Square W1

The Pig and Whistle, Little Chester Street SW1. This name, although often associated with public houses, does not seem to have had a lengthy origin. Even so, suggestions are that it was derived from the Anglo-Saxon *piggen* or *pig* (milking pail) and *wassail* (good health). Another explanation is that it relates to a drinking vessel shaped like a pig so to drink from it was to, 'whet one's whistle'.

The Pig's Ear, Flood Street SW3. The first pub was built in the seventeenth century and was called the **Black Lion**. It was rebuilt in 1892 and later became the **Front Page**. The present refurbishment has produced a sign with a pig dressed in black coat and hat and a brown muffler.

Pillars of Hercules, Greek Street W1. The mythological pillars of Hercules are said to be the rocks at the entrance to the Mediterranean, to the north the Rock of Gibraltar, to the south Mount Hacho. The legendary Hercules created these from one rock, which he broke apart. The sign on this pub, however, depicts the torso of the god pushing one classical pillar while placing his back against the other. The **Hercules Pillars**, Great Queen Street WC2 depicts the god more as a cartoon character pulling a rock after him.

The Pineapple, Leverton Street NW5. The pub was built in 1868. Pineapples were once rare in England and the gift of one was seen as a symbol of generosity. The interior has pineapple symbols on lamps, pots and other ephemera. There is a stone pineapple on the exterior.

The Pint Pot, Tottenham Court Road W1 has an explanatory sign of a publican sitting in his cellar with his barrels holding up a pint pot.

The Place House Tavern, Catford Road SE6. The pub stands on or near the site of the former Place House and the sign shows a reasonable picture of what the house may have been like copied from an old picture. Place House, first mentioned in 1331, is believed to have been the manor house of Sydenham or Sippenham as it was then called.

The Plough, Museum Street WC1 has a sign showing two shire horses pulling a plough.

The Plumber's Arms, Lower Belgrave Street SW1. The sign depicts the arms of the Worshipful Company of Plumbers. The pub, dating from 1821, was built by Thomas Cubbitt, who built much of the surrounding area, but it obtained notoriety in 1974 when Veronica, wife of Lord Lucan, sought help here after she and her nanny, who was killed, were attacked by the earl.

Plume of Feathers. (*See* **Prince of Wales**.)

Pontefract Castle, Wigmore Street W1. The sign depicts a stylised castle on wavy blue and white lines set within a white shield.

Popinjay, Fleet Street EC4. The pub, opened in 1976, had a sign of the bird. It has now been closed and the site given to a café, now closed, but the name is worth recoding because it was on the site of a thirteenth-century house once called the Popyngaye, which belonged to the Abbot of Chichester. In the medieval period there was an annual festival at which archers would shoot at a wooden bird set on a pole. The winner became Captain Popinjay.

Porcupine, Charing Cross Road WC2. This pub is noted on the 1870 Ordnance Survey map. It was a meeting house for the Freemasons until 1827 when it bizarrely banned alcohol at meetings. The sign depicts the rodent armed with its quills as it might appear in a coat of arms. The name can also refer to machines that have a large number of protruding spikes used for mashing during brewing.

Portobello Star, Portobello Road W1. This pub has a sign showing a three-decker ship that refers to the attack by Admiral Vernon on Porto Bello in Panama in 1739 to defeat the French and Spanish fleets. A farm in this area was named to honour the victory.

The Pride of Paddington, Craven Road W2. The sign depicts an early railway steam engine. None were given this name and the sign refers to the pride felt for the nearby Paddington Station.

Prince Albert, Royal Hill SE10 has a sign showing the prince in civilian dress and the **Prince Albert**, Colombo Street SE1 has a sign showing the prince in military dress. Prince Albert (1819-61) was the second son of Ernest, Duke of Saxe-Coburg-Gotha who, from an early age, was groomed to become the husband of Queen Victoria. He married her in 1840 and was created Prince Consort in 1859. At first he was unpopular but just before his death from typhoid his popularity grew. Numerous pubs in London are named after him.

Above left: *Portobello Star, Portobello Road W1*

Above right: *The Pride of Paddington, W1*

Right: *Prince Albert, Royal Hill SE10*

Prince Alfred, Sydenham Road SE26, Pembridge Road W11 and Queensway W2. Prince Alfred (1844-1900), second son of Queen Victoria, was created Duke of Edinburgh on his marriage to the Grand Duchess Marie of Russia. In 1862 he declined an invitation to become King of Greece and in 1867 was wounded in an assassination attempt in Sydney. In Sydenham there are two signs: one depicts a portrait of the prince and the other his coat of arms. **Prince Alfred**, Formosa Street W9 is a mid-Victorian pub with original fittings. The bowed front has etched glass and the interior still has glassed partitions. Access is gained by five separate entrances so that the respective classes in Victorian England could remain separate.

Prince Arthur, Eversholt Street NW1. Royal Mail sorting office staff, engine drivers and guards from Euston Station once frequented this pub. The former sign depicted the eldest son of Henry VII who died in 1502 allowing his younger brother, Henry, to become Henry VIII.

The Prince Bonaparte, Chepstow Road W2 commemorates the Bonaparte dynasty which ruled France under Napoleon I from 1804 to 1815 and again under Napoleon III from 1852 to 1870. The sign displays a bee, which was the symbol of the Bonaparte family.

The Prince Edward, Princes Square W2. The sign depicts the eldest son of Victoria in military uniform and his robes for the House of Lords.

The Prince of Teck, Earls Court Road SW5 refers to the younger brother of Queen Mary who, before her marriage to George V, was Princess of Teck. His Serene Highness Alexander, Prince of Teck in Wurtemburg, (1874-1957) relinquished his title in 1917 and became the first Earl of Athlone. He was Governor General successively of South Africa and of Canada.

Prince of Wales Feathers, Warren Street W1

Prince of Wales, Wilton Street SW1. The sign depicts Edward Prince of Wales, later Edward VII in military uniform and wearing his House of Lords robes. A plume of three ostrich feathers is the sign which usually indicates a **Prince of Wales** public house. Edward, Prince of Wales (1330-1376), eldest son of Edward III, known as the Black Prince, adopted the feathers as his distinctive crest, together with the motto *Ich Dien* ('I serve'), after the Battle of Poitiers in 1356. The sign of the **Prince of Wales Feathers**, Warren Street W1 shows the crest in splendid array, as do those of the **Prince of Wales** public houses in Perry Rise SE26, Kensington Church Street, W8, Willesden Lane NW6, Clapham Old Town SW4 and Drury Lane WC2. The **Plume of Feathers** is also a common pub sign. One of the best signs is at Park Vista SE10 on one of the oldest pubs in Greenwich. The abbreviated sign the **Feathers**, Broadway SW1 also indicates loyalty to the crown.

Prince William Henry, Blackfriars Road SE1. The portrait sign refers to one of two princes. Prince William Henry (1743-1805), the son of Frederick, Prince of Wales, and grandson of George

II, was created Duke of Gloucester on the accession of his elder brother George III to the throne in 1760. He secretly married Maria Walpole, Duchess of Waldegrave, in 1766, which act contributed to the Royal Marriages Act (1772) whereby it was illegal for a member of the royal family to marry without the approval of the sovereign. Another Prince William Henry, (1765- 1837), Duke of Clarence, was the third son of George III. He served in the Royal Navy and was known as the Sailor King when he inherited the throne as William IV in 1830. He died in 1837.

The Princess Alice, Romford Road E7 and the **Princess Alice**, Commercial Street E1 both commemorate the disastrous sinking of the pleasure boat, the *Princess Alice*, which after returning from a day's outing collided with the *Bywell Castle*, a collier boat. Although only 300 yards from the shore not many people could swim and at least 640 people were drowned. As the disaster happened near to the outfall of untreated sewage into the Thames, many probably died from swimming in the foul water. The Romford Road pub was destroyed in the London Blitz but was rebuilt and the name perpetuated.

Princess Louise, High Holborn WC1. The sign depicts the fourth daughter of Queen Victoria and wife of the Duke of Argyll. The pub was built in 1872 and has a protection order on it because of its excellent interior fittings, including tiles by Arthur Chitty and glasswork by R. Morris and Sons. There is a magnificent horseshoe bar with an original clock and mirrors.

The Princess of Prussia, Prescot Street E1. The sign depicts a woman in a blue dress with a white headdress. The princess referred to is the probably the eldest daughter of Queen Victoria who married Frederick, eldest son of Wilhelm I, King of Prussia in 1858. Wilhelm became Emperor of Germany in 1871; Frederick succeeded him in 1888 but died of cancer of the throat ninety-nine days later leaving his son Wilhelm II to become King of Prussia and Emperor of Germany.

The Princess of Wales, Villiers Street WC2 displays a sign showing the Danish Princess. **Princess of Wales**, Chalcot Street NW1 was believed to have been named to commemorate the wedding of Princess Alexandra and the future Edward VII in 1863. In 1944 it was renamed the **Swan at Coole** after W.B. Yeats poem *Wild Swans at Coole*. Yeats lived on Fitzroy Road 1863-73 and presumably frequented the pub. It was renamed **Princess of Wales** in 1997 (*See* the **Alexandra**). The **Princess of Wales**, Montpellier Row SE3 is a large eighteenth-century pub named after Princess Caroline of Brunswick (1768-1821), who married George IV, when he was Prince of Wales in 1795. The prince disliked her intensely and they separated the next year. She refused to divorce him and subsequently became Queen though George barred her from his Coronation. The pub is noted for the fact that it was here that the first rugby international was planned in 1871. Blackheath Rugby Club uses the pub as its headquarters and changing rooms.

Prince of Wales, Wilton Street SW1

Prince Regent, Nottingham Street W1. The sign shows a profile of the eldest son of George III, who became George IV (1820-30). He was created Prince Regent in 1811 when George IIIs insanity became obvious. Although he has been described as selfish, indulgent and a bad husband, father and friend, his patronage of the arts contributed to England's cultural inheritance. The **Prince Regent**, Gloucester Road SW7 has a handsome sign of the prince. This pub used to be the **Black Widow**.

The Printer Devil, Fetter Lane EC4. A printer's devil was an errand boy who also did odd jobs. A previous sign showed a horned devil tossing letters about from a text. The present one depicts the printer with an old fashioned press taking an axe to his printer's devil who has upset some liquid on the floor.

The Priory Tavern, Belsize Road NW6. The sign is a tonsured friar standing in front of a church. This refers to the Augustinian Priory, which was dissolved in 1536 at the Reformation. *Abbey Road* of Beatles' fame is named after it.

The Prospect of Whitby, Wapping Wall E1. This is probably one of the most famous pubs in London. It is reputed to be London's oldest riverside pub having been developed from a 1520 farmhouse. The pub was originally called the **Devil's Tavern** because of its association with smugglers and thieves, but it was gutted by fire in 1682. In the next century it changed its name to that of a collier boat *The Prospect* from Whitby, which used to moor nearby. Samuel Pepys drank here when he was in Wapping on naval business as secretary to the Admiralty. It is one of the pubs claiming to be that which Charles Dickens used as 'The Six Jolly Fellowship Porters' in *Our Mutual Friend* (*See* the **Grapes**). The long bar has a stone-flagged interior and the walls are lined with photographs of Thames water life. The pub lies along the river and a noose hanging outside may refer to executions, which took place nearby, or to the hanging Judge Jeffreys, who often drank here but who was apprehended at the nearby Town of Ramsgate when trying to flee the country in 1688. He had presided over the Bloody Assizes in Winchester, which tried those who had taken part in the Monmouth Rebellion in 1685, when the Duke of Monmouth attempted to gain the throne from James II. (*See* colour picture 22.)

Punch & Judy, Covent Garden WC2. This sign shows these exuberant characters and refers to the entertainments taking place in the market. On the first Sunday in October each year Punch and Judy puppeteers (or professors as they prefer to be called) gather in the piazza to entertain the crowds. Punch and Judy have a long history. On 9 May 1662 Samuel Pepys noted in his diary that he saw an 'Italian puppet play' outside St Paul's church at Covent Garden which probably refers to a Punch and Judy show. He liked it so much that he returned at least three times to see it, bringing friends with him. (*See* colour picture 23.)

The Punch Tavern, Fleet Street EC4, with a profile sign of Mr Punch, is a Victorian pub, built in 1841 and decorated inside with the dual nature of Punch – Punch and Judy memorabilia and *Punch* Magazine. The latter commemorates the fact that the staff of that magazine used to meet in the pub until the magazine closed in 1992. Its previous name was the **Crown and Sugar Loaf**. The pub had an entrance from Bride Lane but a wall was built up between the two bars and the **Crown and Sugar Loaf** is now in Bride Lane.

Queen Adelaide, Putney Bridge Road, SW18. Queen Adelaide was the wife of William IV. The sign shows the queen's head as if in an open locket.

The Queen's Arms, Kilburn High Road NW6. The sign shows the portrait of a queen who might be Elizabeth I with arms reaching up to her, thereby creating a clever punning sign.

Queens Head. This is a popular sign and most, as do those in Denman Street W1 and Theobalds Road WC1 show a profile of Queen Victoria in her old age, with her white flowing headdress and black gown. The Denman Street pub was first named in 1738 and the landlord operated both as a seller of wines and brandy and as a coal merchant. The house was rebuilt in 1928 and is now part of the Piccadilly Theatre. **The Queens Head**, Tryon Street SW3 has a painting of what may purport to be Victoria but more resembles a Spanish lady wearing a black gown. On her head is a white veil held in place with a gold tiara. The **Queens Head**, Black Prince Road SE1 uses the penny black stamp as its sign.

The Queens Larder, Queen Square WC1. The original sign depicted a queen bearing food to a larder while the knave looks on. The present one shows the queen opening the door to an empty larder while a disappointed dog looks on. The name refers to the

Queen Adelaide, Putney Bridge Road SW18

Queens Head, Theobalds Road WC1

time when Dr Willis in Queen Square treated George III, during one of his periodic bouts of illness. His wife, Queen Charlotte, is said to have rented part of the cellar at this nearby inn so that she could store provisions there. (*See* colour picture 24.)

R

The Railway. This sign did not appear until the mid-nineteenth century but then became very common. Many pubs were situated by railway stations to serve travellers or the navvies who built the railways. Surprisingly London has not as many as may be expected. The **Railway**, Sydenham Road SE26 was built after the Croydon Canal was drained and converted to the London & Croydon Railway in the 1840s. The **Railway**, Upper Richmond Road SW15 is a huge Victorian corner pub sporting a sign of a steam engine, as does the **Railway Tavern**, Crouch End Hill N8, a 1930s mock Tudor-style building. The **Railway Tavern**, Liverpool Street EC2 has a fine sign incorporating *The Flying Scotsman*. The walls of the pub are lined with photos of Liverpool Street Station. The **Railway Tavern**, Blackheath Village SE3 shows an engine drawing coaches with lighted windows, racing along through the night under a full moon. The **Railway Telegraph**, Stanstead Road SE23 depicts engine number 46425 racing along belching out black fumes. The **Railway Bell**, Cawnpore Road SE19 has a sign showing a hand pulling a rope to sound the bell while a streamlined train runs by.

The Raven in the Tower, Tower Bridge Road SE1 is now awaiting refurbishment or even demolition but its proximity to the Tower of London recalls the legend that if ravens leave the tower it will fall and the monarchy will be deposed. The ravens therefore have their wings clipped to prevent them flying away.

The Railway Tavern, Liverpool Street EC2

The Red Lion, Crown Passage SW1

Red Lion. This is one of the most popular signs for pubs. It was the badge of John of Gaunt (1340-99), fourth son of Edward III, created Duke of Lancaster in 1362, who unofficially ruled for his senile father for the latter part of the King's reign. His unpopularity contributed to the 1381 Peasant's Revolt when his home, the Savoy Palace in London was destroyed. The Red Lion may also be a heraldic reference to James VI of Scotland, who, on inheriting the English throne, became James I of England in 1603. When he succeeded, it became politic to put the heraldic red lion of Scotland on inn signs. The sign is usually displayed as a lion rampant (on its hind legs) as shown on most pub signs like those in Great Windmill Street W1 and Waverton Street W1. The **Red Lion** in Parliament

Street SW1, a nineteenth-century building on the site of one built in 1733, has a division bell for MPs and pictures of prime ministers cover the walls. This pub is one of many in the area, which on the nearest Sunday to 30 January are flooded with members of the Sealed Knot Society and other re-enactment societies commemorating the execution of Charles I in 1649. The **Red Lion**, Duke of York Street SW1 is a very small pub with coloured prints of the area. Built in 1821 and refurbished in the 1870s, it still retains its splendid glass and woodwork. The **Red Lion**, Crown Passage SW1 claims to be the second oldest pub in the West End. This small pub has prints of the Whitehall and the St James area, and Punch cartoons. The **Red Lion**, Kilburn High Road NW6 was built in the nineteenth century on the site of a much earlier pub. This house, used by coaches travelling along Watling Street and the Great North Road, was also a tollhouse and a prison and was a venue for the manorial courts. The **Red Lion**, St Mary's Road W5, which dates back to the eighteenth century, is opposite Ealing Studios and numerous film stars of the *Ealing Comedies* drank here between scenes. The frontage, with the handsome red lion resting on the parapet, was added in the nineteenth century. Note also the iron lions on the floor bar rail.

Richard I, Royal Hill SE10. The hill was originally known as Gang Lane as it was the haunt of press gangs that raided the pubs to press men into the navy. The sign shows the king dressed in a surcoat with the royal arms and wielding a sword. Richard reigned from 1189 to 1199 but for most of his reign he was fighting in other countries. In 1190 he went on the Third Crusade, was taken prisoner on his return by Leopold II of Austria and incarcerated in Durnstein Castle on the Danube until a ransom was paid.

The Ring, Blackfriars Road SE1 has an upper floor in which is a small gym. It stands opposite the original site of the **Southwark Ring**, formerly the Surrey Chapel (where now is the tube station) which was bombed in 1940. The present pub sign says that the latter place was where boxing began in 1810.

The Rising Sun is a very common sign. It was the heraldic sign of Edward III and Richard III although the sign is more likely to be akin to that of the **Rising Sun** sign in Lewisham High Street SE 13, which displays an idyllic scene. The **Rising Sun Cloth Fair**, EC1 has spiky rays representing the rising sun. The pub was reputed to be one of the haunts of the Resurrection Men who stole newly buried bodies from the nearby graveyards of St Bartholomew the Great and St Andrews and sold them to surgeons at St Bartholomew's. The Rising Sun is also the crest of the Distillers Co. As the pub is near St Bartholomew's church it is fitting that prints of the church are on the walls of the pub. The **Rising Sun**, Carter Lane EC4 stands on the site of the **Hart's Horn** where the conspirators of the Gunpowder Plot are reputed to have met.

Rob Roy, Sale Place W2 has a sign showing a highlander. Rob Roy, whose real name was Rob Roy Macgregor (1671-1734), was a member of the proscribed Macgregor clan. He made a living cattle droving but became an outlaw in 1712 when the Marquis of Montrose advanced him £1,000 that was stolen by an associate, leaving Rob Roy to be accused of theft. He therefore began raiding cattle from the herds of the Montrose. After voluntarily giving himself up, he was pardoned in 1727 and died peacefully at his home in Balquhidder. He is the hero or anti-hero of the novel, *Rob Roy* (1818) by Sir Walter Scott.

The Robert Browning, Clifton Road W9. Originally called the **Eagle**, this pub was renamed after the poet and displays his portrait on the sign. The poet lived in Warwick Crescent nearby and there are some stained glass windows depicting both the poet and his wife, Elizabeth Barrett Browning.

The Rocket, Churchfield Road W3 is a modern pub but the sign is an interesting one showing a Victorian family – man, woman and child – admiring Robert Stephenson's *Rocket* engine.

The Roebuck is more often to be found in country towns. Its appearance in Great Dover Street SW1 and Pond Street NW3 may, therefore, be a surprise. The roebuck is a species of the roe deer, the small species of spotted deer.

The Rose & Crown was a sign depicting loyalty to the monarchy and has been popular since the sixteenth century. It was associated with Henry VII and his Queen. Henry VII had won his throne at the Battle of Bosworth in 1485 but as his descent to the throne was somewhat difficult, he had to legitimise it. This he did by marrying Elizabeth of York, daughter of Edward IV, whose beauty had given her the appellation of the Rose of York. The crown of England (Henry) was thus forever associated with the white rose of York (Elizabeth) and symbolised the end of the Wars of the Roses. The **Rose & Crown**, High Street SW19 traces its origins back to the seventeenth century when it was known as the **Sign of the Rose**. The sign displays the combined white rose of York and the red rose of Lancaster, together with the crowned head of a monarch. The Victorian poet Algernon Swinburne (1837-1909) frequently drank here though he used a private room to avoid the crowds. The **Rose & Crown**, Wandsworth High Street SW18 has a rose placed in a medieval crown. The **Rose & Crown**, Crooms Hill SE10 has the rose and the crown side by side. The **Rose & Crown**, Colombo Street SE1 has a more elaborate sign of a rose entwined within the crown. The **Rose & Crown**, Crown Lane SW16 has the imperial crown resting on a cushion with a handsome rose beside it. (*See* colour picture 25.)

The Rose of Denmark, Cross Street SW13 refers to the title given to Queen Alexandra (*See* the **Alexandra**) who inaugurated the Alexandra Rose day in 1912 to mark the fifty years since her arrival in England. Rose emblems were sold to raise money for hospitals.

The Rosemary Branch, Shepperton Road N1. This pub is built on the site of one first established in 1783. Rosemary, depicted on the sign, as a symbol of faithfulness and remembrance, was used as decoration at weddings and funerals. The pub is a theatre pub but its great days were when it was a music hall. Now it is also a venue for artists to display their wares.

Round Table, St Martin's Court WC2. The sign depicts a round table. This pub was originally called **Ben Gaunt's Head** after the Yorkshire prizefighter who arranged fights for viewing by the nobility in the early nineteenth century. The sign of the round table ensured that fights took place with no cheating. The present building dates from 1877 when the area was partly developed to create Charing Cross Road between Oxford Street and Charing Cross. The land was bought by Sir Charles Wyndham, the actor manager, who built the Wyndham and Albery Theatres named respectively after Sir Charles and his stepson.

The Roundhouse, Garrick Street WC2. This pub opened in 1868 as **Petter's Hotel** and served theatre goers and also market porters and traders, until the Covent Garden Market moved to Nine Elms. In 1943 it was renamed the **Roundhouse** ostensibly because that was its shape, although the accrual shape is a semi-circle. The sign is a roundhouse.

The Royal Exchange. The sign for this pub in Sale Place W2 is not what might be expected. The sign depicts a desperate King Richard III reduced to kneeling before a bewildered country yokel pleading for a horse, the obvious reference being to the quotation in Shakespeare's *Richard III* (Act 5, sc. IV), 'A horse, a horse, my kingdom for a horse'.

The Royal George, Blissett Street SE10. The pub sign depicts a three-masted ship firing a broadside. The *Royal George*, first laid down as the *Royal Anne* but renamed in 1758 in honour of George II, took part in the Seven Years' War in a blockade of the port of Brest. She was sent to Spithead for repairs in 1782, but capsized and sank quickly with the loss of 600 men, 300 women and sixty children who were visiting her at the time. The exact cause of the capsize is not known but one suggestion is that she keeled over too far and that water entered her gun ports. This disaster did not prevent the name being used on later ships. The **Royal George**, Eversholt Street NW1 has a similar sign. The **Royal George**, Goslett Yard WC2 is a new pub where the sign is a bust of George III painted blue.

The Royal Oak is a very popular sign, probably only secondary to the Red Lion. After Charles I was executed in 1649 his son Charles II tried to reclaim the throne but was defeated at the Battle of Worcester in 1651. To escape his pursuers, Charles and his companion, Colonel Careless, hid in an oak tree at Boscobel, near Shifnel, Shropshire from noon to dusk. When Charles was restored as king in 1660, it was decreed that 29 May, the King's birthday, should be proclaimed as Oak Apple Day or Royal Oak Day in thanksgiving for the King's escape. The usual sign, as at the **Royal Oak**, Oakfield Road SE20 depicts a crown in the middle of an oak tree. The **Royal Oak**, Tabard Street SE1 is a bare floor-boarded pub with much etched glass and mahogany. The sign shows the King, in the branches of the tree, peering down on his pursuers.

The Royal Standard, High Street, Colliers Wood SW19 has two signs. One shows the Royal Standard flag flying at the masthead, the other a coat of arms of the Royal Standard with flags on either side. The Royal Standard is the personal standard of the sovereign and is only flown when he or she is present.

The Rugby Tavern, Great James Street WC1 takes its name from the nearby Rugby Street and the fact that much of the area was once owned by Rugby School. The theme of the pub is obviously the game with photographs, scorecards and other sporting memorabilia. The sign shows a huge rugby ball about to be kicked over the goal posts. Inside is an older sign showing a rugby player about to kick the ball. (*See* colour picture 26.)

Royal George, Eversholt Street NW1

The Royal Oak, Oakfield Street SE20

The Royal Oak, Tabard Street SE1

The Running Footman, Charles Street W1

The Running Footman, Charles Street W1. Important persons employed a footman to run in front of their coaches to check that the way was not too rough or to announce their arrival. Charles Perrault used this theme in his fairy tale *Puss in Boots* who announces that his master, the Marquis of Carabas was coming. In Mayfair, running footmen congregated at this pub in Charles Street, which became known as the **Running Footman**. The title was changed to **I am the Only Running Footman** in honour of the last remaining running footman in the service of the fourth Marquess of Queensberry (Old Q; died 1810). The original sign had a portrait of him. Subsequent signs have depicted a man running before a coach.

The Running Horse, Davies Street W1. The sign is a double one. On one side is a jockey racing his horse towards the winning post and on the other a woman riding sidesaddle through the desert.

S

The Salisbury, St Martin's Lane WC2 bears a fine sign of Robert Arthur Talbot Gascoyne-Cecil, third Marquis of Salisbury (1830-1903), who was prime minister three times (1885, 1886-92, 1892-1902) and his own foreign minister during the reign of Queen Victoria. This pub, rebuilt in 1898, was originally called the **Coach and Horses** and later the **Ben Gaunt's Head** after a Yorkshire prizefighter, a landlord in the early nineteenth century (*See* **Round Table**). It takes its name from the fact that it stands on land leased from the Salisbury family. The Cecil coat of arms is placed over the door. The splendid interior is well worth seeing for the Art Nouveau light fittings and the huge etched mirrors. It is probably one of the greatest untouched survivals of the Victorian gin palace.

The Samuel Johnson, Mitcham Lane SW16. Samuel Johnson (1709-84) is best known as the compiler of *A Dictionary of the English Language*, which was not the first English dictionary but perhaps the most comprehensible. He also wrote several novels and edited Shakespeare's plays. The presence of the name in this area relates to the fact that Johnson was a frequent visitor to Streatham Park, the home of his close friend and patron, Mrs Thrale, who was the wife of the brewer Henry Thrale MP for Southwark in the 1770s.

The Samuel Pepys, Clarges Street W1 shows the keeper of the diary on its sign. Pepys (1633-1703), the naval official secretary to

The Samuel Pepys, Clarges Street W1

the admiralty kept a diary, which he wrote in cipher and which was finally published in 1825. It describes in detail life in the 1660s.

The Sawyers Arms, London Street W2 is a punning sign showing two strapping lads sawing a huge oak log.

Scarborough Arms, St Mark Street E1. The sign depicts the arms of the Scarborough family on a shield argent, a *fesse gules*, between three birds, breast or, wings and back vert. The Earl of Scarborough fought against the rebel army of the Duke of Monmouth at the Battle of Sedgemoor in 1685.

The Scarsdale, Edwards Square W8. The pub is set in the corner of the square built between 1811-19 by the Frenchman Louis Léon Changeur, reputedly to house French officers in the event of a successful invasion. The pub was intended to be an officers' mess.

The Sekforde Arms, Sekforde Street EC1, built in 1835, is named after Thomas Sekforde, a lawyer, who was a patron of Saxton, the cartographer who produced maps and the first county atlas in the sixteenth century. On the walls of the pub are the arms of the Sekforde family. There is a splendid collection of used champagne bottles inside.

Serjeant's, Old Mitre Court EC4. The pub, neatly tucked away off Fleet Street, was rebuilt after it was destroyed in the 1941 Blitz and is named after Serjeant's Inn, one of the Inns of Court. The sign shows a reconstructed appearance of what purports to be the original site.

Seven Stars, Carey Street WC2. This unspoilt pub dates back to the early seventeenth century and was originally known as the **League of Seven Stars** in a bid to attract Dutch sailors as the stars may represent the seven provinces of the Netherlands. The seven stars, which are displayed on the sign, were also a religious symbol, and an astrological sign as can be seen in the Plough and the sign was adopted by the Innkeepers Company. Inside the pub are caricatures of famous lawyers. The low-beamed interior retains its narrow settles and legal film posters. The clientele, as expected, is often from the nearby law courts.

Shakespeare's Head, Great Marlborough Street W1. The pub has two signs. The painted sign, a reproduction of Martin Droeshouts' portrait, depicts the playwright with green doublet and white collar, but a bust of Shakespeare leans out of an alcove watching the scene below. Close inspection reveals that one hand is missing, a casualty of Second World War bomb damage. The **Shakespeare's Head**, Arlington Way EC1 and the **Shakespeare**, Westbourne Grove W2 both display signs with the head of the great Elizabethan dramatist.

Seven Stars, Carey Street WC2

*Shakespeare's Head, Great
Marlborough Street W1*

Shepherd's Tavern, Hertford Street W1 relates to Edward Shepherd, a property owner, who founded the pub and created Shepherd Market in 1735, thereby creating a delightful enclave off Piccadilly.

The Sherlock Holmes, Northumberland Avenue WC2. This pub, which houses the Sherlock Holmes Museum, is dedicated to memorabilia of the great detective including a reconstruction of his room in 221B Baker Street. Engraved glass windows have portraits of Sherlock Holmes, Dr Watson and Sir Arthur Conan Doyle. It is perhaps a coincidence that Sir Henry Baskerville (in the story *The Hound of the Baskervilles*) stayed in the Northumberland Hotel once situated nearby.

The Ship. There are many pubs called the Ship in London. Most, such as those in Borough High Street SE1, Kennington Park Road, SE1, Wardour Street W1 and Kensington High Road SE1 have a sign depicting a sailing ship in full sail. The **Ship**, Thames Bank

SW14 is worth visiting to see the nautical prints displayed in its interior. The **Ship**, Talbot Court EC3 is a Victorian pub in the courtyard of a former coaching inn. The **Ship**, Jew's Row SW18, built in the early nineteenth century is a typical riverside pub used by watermen and those who plied their trade on the Thames. The **Ship Tavern**, Gate Street WC1 has three signs, two hanging and one placed over the door, all of three-masted, sixteenth-century ships in full sail flying the cross of St George. Two have an heraldic red lion and a cross on separate sails. This pub claims to date from 1549 but was rebuilt in the 1920s: some stained glass remains from that time. After the Reformation it was used by Catholic priests to hold masses and still has several priest holes. In the eighteenth century the Freemasons used it after the Grand Master, the Earl of Antrim, had consecrated it in 1786.

Ship Tavern, Gate Street WC1

Ship & Shovel, Craven Passage WC2. This pub, which dates back to at least 1707, has the distinction of having two parts, one on each side of the passage. The sign depicts a portrait of the Admiral Sir Cloudsley Shovel. It is reputed that in Queen Anne's reign, he frequented the pub so often that people went to the **Ship** to seek Shovel, hence the name. His fleet was wrecked off the Scilly Isles in 1707. Even though the admiral survived the shipwreck, he was killed by one of the islanders. However, a second meaning of the name refers to the men who shovelled grain and coal into ships. When they entered a pub they were asked to leave their shovels outside.

Shipwrights Arms, Tooley Street SE1 has a nautical theme with a mural of shipbuilding and a model sailing ship. The Worshipful Company of Shipwrights was incorporated in 1606. The sign of the door is a ship's figurehead of a woman.

The Shooting Star, Middlesex Street E1 has no sign but is worth a mention as from 1896 to 1956 it housed the Board of Guardians and Trustees for the relief of the Jewish poor in this area of London. A plaque to commemorate this was set up in 1989 and unveiled by the Lord Mayor of London. Middlesex Street is also Petticoat Lane, so called because second-hand and indeed fourth-hand clothing was sold here. The market still takes place on Sundays.

Sir Alexander Fleming, St Michael's Street W2. This pub was originally called The Polly Perkins relating the rhyme of *Pretty Polly Perkins of Paddington Green*. When the pub passed from one landlord to his daughter, she renamed the pub to commemorate Sir Alexander Fleming who discovered penicillin at the nearby St Mary's Hospital. The sign depicts Fleming with a book recalling his discovery. (*See* colour picture 27.)

Sir Alfred Hitchcock, Whipps Cross Road E11 commemorates the film producer who was born in Leytonstone in 1899. The hotel-pub's memorabilia on the walls included copies of Hitchcock's birth and marriage certificates, and photographs and posters relating to his films.

Sir Christopher Hatton, Leather Lane EC1. This pub, which had a fine sign of a painting of Sir Christopher, has now been taken over by the Goose Chain and the sign has gone, but it is worth mentioning because the pub stands on land, which was rented to Sir Christopher by the Bishop of Ely. This covered the area now known as Hatton Gardens.

Sir Colin Campbell, Kilburn High Road NW6 has a sign showing the general in Scots bonnet and plaid jacket. (*See* **Lord Clyde**.)

The Sir Richard Steele, Haverstock Hill NW3, built in the 1870s was named after an Irish ex-soldier, poet and essayist, and briefly a MP, who lived in the vicinity and was the founder of *The Spectator* and *The Tatler*. His image is inside the pub rather than on the outside.

Sir Robert Peel, Langdale Close SE17 is named after the great statesman and twice prime minister (1799-1850) who secured the Catholic Emancipation Act (1829), created the London Police Force (1829) and whose policies gave rise to the modern Conservative party. **Sir Robert Peel**, Bishopsgate EC2. This pub is now a food outlet but from a viewpoint outside Liverpool Street Station the name and the portrait of the statesman can been seen on the upper part of the building.

Sir Walter Scott, Broadway Market E8, built in 1909 by the side of the Grand Union Canal has now become **La Vie en Rose**.

The Skinners Arms, Judd Street WC1. The Skinners Co., which had its first charter granted in 1327, controlled the fur trade in England until the eighteenth century. It also has had a

close connection with education providing funds for a variety
of schools. Sir Andrew Judd, who was five times master in the
sixteenth century, founded Tonbridge School. A previous **Skinners
Arms** in Great Suffolk Street SE1, which had a sign showing
the arms of the Worshipful Company of Skinners, is now the
Town House.

Spaniard's Inn, Spaniards Road, NW3 was built in the late
sixteenth century and became an inn 200 years later. The name
comes either from the Count of Gondomar, the Spanish Ambassador
to James I's court, who had a residence here, or to the landlords, two
Spanish brothers, Francesco and Juan Porero, who fought a dual
over a lady. It is reputed that Juan lost and is buried in the garden.
His ghost joins that of Dick Turpin who possibly used the inn as a
hideout. Jack Shepherd, another highwayman also used the inn as
a base, as did some of the participants in the 1780 Gordon Riots.
The poet Keats also frequented the inn. Dickens mentioned it in
The Pickwick Papers and numerous poets and writers who lived in
Hampstead used it as their local.

Spanish Galleon, Greenwich Church Street SE10. The pub sign
shows a three-masted galleon in full sail. The name probably alludes
to ships of the Spanish Armada (1588). The pub was first built in the
reign of William IV (1830-39). In the bar is a nineteenth-century
sailor's uniform, which was found in a bricked-up room when the
pub was renovated in 1985.

The Spice Island, Rotherhithe Street SE16 is a barn-like pub built
to resemble the wooden warehouses in which spices were stored.
There is a good view from the terrace across the river.

Spinnaker, Harbour Exchange Square E14. A spinnaker is a large
triangular sail used by racing yachts and the maritime pictures on
the windows of the pub indicate this.

Spread Eagle, Wandsworth
High Street SW18

Spread Eagle, Wandsworth High Street SW18 dates from the eighteenth century when it was an important coaching inn. It was rebuilt in the nineteenth century and retains many of its magnificent features, including a tearoom and a dance hall although these are not used for their original purpose. The sign depicts the shadow of an eagle swooping over a hare, which flees in terror across a field. The **Spread Eagle**, Albert Street NW1 depicts the eagle with outspread wings swooping over fields in the twilight.

St Bride's Tavern, Bridewell Place EC4 has on its sign the nearby St Bride's church. This was built (1670–84) by Sir Christopher Wren. It was gutted in the bombing of 1940 and refurbished by Godfrey Adam. The tiered wedding cake is said to have been inspired by the church steeple.

St Christopher Inn, Greenwich High Road SE10. This pub has the Greenwich Theatre attached to it. It was originally known as the **Prince of Orange** but the present name of the saint who protects travellers is very appropriate as the pub is next to Greenwich Station.

St Paul's Tavern, Chiswell Street EC1. This pub, which occupies a long frontage of four Georgian houses, claims to have been founded in 1736. The sign (now gone) displayed St Paul's Cathedral.

St Stephen's Tavern, Bridge Street SW1 originally built in 1867, was then called the **Swan Tavern**. It got its present name from the clock tower, St Stephen's Tower, or the clock tower containing Big Ben. At one time it was almost totally frequented by MPs and their guests.

The Stage Door, Webber Street SE1

The Stage Door, Webber Street SE1. This pub is near to the Old Vic so it is not surprising that the sign shows two white masks on a plain background. One depicts comedy with the mouth turned upward, the other tragedy with the mouth turned down. The **Stage Door**, Allington Street SW1 has more theatres surrounding it. It has recently been refitted and lost some of its charm although it retained some pictures of the surroundings of Victoria. The sign depicts what might be a stage door Johnny waiting for a chorus girl.

Stanhope Arms, Gloucester Road SW7. This handsome Victorian pub has the arms of a branch of the Stanhope family set over the door.

The Star, Belgrave Mews West SW1 was built in the nineteenth century to serve the staff who served the nobility in the surrounding area.

Star & Garter, Poland Street W1. The sign depicts the insignia of the Garter: the Star and the Garter with the motto inscribed on it. The Order of the Garter, which is in the personal gift of the sovereign and limited to members of the Royal Family and twenty-five knights, has its origin in legend. It is said that Edward III retrieved a garter dropped by the Countess of Shrewsbury. To silence the leering courtiers he declared, *Honi soit qui mal y pense* (evil be to he who evil thinks). This was adopted as the motto of the Order.

Still & Star, Somerset Street E1 has a name commemorating the still used in a distilling process. As butchers frequented this pub in the late nineteenth century it came under the surveillance of the police who believed that Jack the Ripper might have been a butcher or a slaughterman.

The Sun in Splendour, Portobello Road W1. The name usually refers to a royal badge. This particular pub is remarkable for having a corridor decorated with a jungle scene reminiscent of those done by the painter Henri Rousseau. This was done by the graffiti artist Alex Martinez.

Surprise, Christchurch Terrace SW3. This pub appears to have changed little from the mid-nineteenth century with its scrubbed tables and wooden settles. The sign denotes a sailing ship being approached by a rowing boat. This probably refers to the boat, which took Charles II to exile in France in 1651 on his escape when he made his way through England after the Battle of Worcester. The sign displays a large naval ship but the actual ship that conveyed the King was a small collier called the *Surprise*. Charles repaid his debt. When he was restored to the throne in 1660 he bought the ship, renamed it *Royal Escape* and used it as the Royal Yacht. The pub has another surprise. A picture inside the pub shows another HMS *Surprise*, which was a French ship, renamed after its capture in 1796. In 1821 the ship conveyed the body of the Emperor Napoleon from St Helena to France where it was interred in the church of the Invalids.

The Sussex, Long Acre WC2 has a long tradition of serving theatre goers and those visiting the crowded area between Leicester Square and Covent Garden. The sign shows the arms of Sussex with mantling and helm.

Sutton Arms, Carthusian Street EC1. The Carthusian monks, who established themselves in London in the thirteenth century, had so strict a rule that only a few houses were founded in England. At the Reformation almost the whole order defied Henry VIII. The prior and the monks of the London Charterhouse were executed and the property was forfeited to the crown. Later it was bought by Sir Thomas Sutton, a courtier of Elizabeth I. As he travelled a great deal and had little use for the priory buildings he founded a school and an almshouse for retired men. Charterhouse School has moved to Godalming, but the almshouse still retains its original purpose today. The nearby public house, where the sign displays his arms, is a reminder of this act of philanthropy.

The Swan. This sign is more unusual in London than in rural England. The **Swan Inn**, with its gracious sign of the bird, in Bayswater Road W2 is reputed to have been established in 1723 when it was one of the first hostelries for travellers approaching London from the west. It stood in a garden belonging to Sir John Hill, which was a popular place of entertainment in the eighteenth century. It is somewhat surprising that the pub still survives along what is one of the main thoroughfares into London. The **Swan Tavern**, Ship Tavern Passage EC3, reputed to be the smallest in the city, is an Edwardian pub. The sign depicts a swan on a blue and red shield. (*See* colour picture 28.)

Swiss Cottage, Finchley Road NW3 was originally built to resemble a Swiss chalet in 1849 next to the tollgate on Finchley Road. The present building is post-Second World War. The Swiss appearance continues inside with its exposed timber walls. The sign depicts two Tyroleans yodelling.

Sydney Arms, Lewisham Road SE13. The sign is a portrait of the Tudor poet Sir Philip Sydney (1554-80). He died at the Battle of Zutphen.

Sydney Arms, Lewisham Road SE13

T

The Tabard, Bath Road W4. The pub was built by Norman Shaw in the arts and crafts style favoured in 1880. As it is on the Bedford Park estate there is a useful map of the estate on the walls together with some William Morris designs. The tabard, worn by heralds, was a short coat with no sleeves, emblazoned with the arms of the sovereign. Knights could also wear tabards over their armour, showing their own coats of arms so that their dignity could be recognised. The most famous **Tabard Inn** was that in Southwark, demolished after a fire in 1676, from which Chaucer's pilgrims in 1388 set out on their journey to Canterbury, 'To Southwark, at the Tabard, as I lay Ready to go on pilgrimage to Canterbury'. The **Tabard**, Chiswick W4 is a theatre pub supposedly haunted by an elderly lady dressed in black.

The Talbot, Tyrwhitt Road SE4 refers to a hound with a very keen sense of smell used for hunting. The **Talbot Tavern**, Little Chester Street SW1 was rebuilt after being bombed in the Second World War.

The Talma, Wells Park Road SE26. This unique pub sign refers to François Joseph Talma (1763-1826) who came to England and became a famous actor. He instituted the custom that an actor should wear the costume appropriate to the period represented in the play.

The Talma, Wells Park Road SE26

Tea Clipper, Montpelier Street SW7. Clipper ships were originally built in the USA but became the fastest type of sailing ship. Many sailed between Europe and the Far East mostly bringing back cargoes of tea. Huge prizes were offered for the ship that could deliver the first cargo of tea in the season. This pub has two signs depicting a ship in full sail.

The Telegraph, Telegraph Road SW15 describes itself as an inn in the country and this is apt as it is on an isolated site on Putney Heath, far away from the noise of London. The sign depicts a house with railway signals but the signals have another function. During the Napoleonic Wars a system of poles and painted boards, (in which this house participated) with running messengers, was devised to send messages from London to Portsmouth. As might be expected this did not work and so in 1821 a system of semaphore houses was arranged, not with great success as these were abandoned over twenty years later.

The Ten Bells, Commercial Street E1 with its sign of a bell with a ten in the centre achieves notoriety from the fact that it is the only pub in the area to have survived from the 1880s and that this was the pub where Mary Kelly, the last of Jack the Ripper's victims spent the last evening of her life having a drink. Cashing in on this in 1970s, the pub's name was changed to **Jack the Ripper** but after the pub sold 'Ripper-Tipples' in the 1980s the name reverted to the **Ten Bells**.

Thomas à Becket, Old Kent Road SE1. This pub had its days of glory when it had an upstairs gym where boxers such as Henry Cooper and Frank Bruno trained and Muhamuad Ali was a frequent visitor. Archbishop Thomas Becket (1117-70) was murdered in Canterbury Cathedral by four knights who had taken to heart Henry II's exasperated words, 'Who will rid me of this turbulent priest'. In 1174 Henry was forced to make penance for this act but the murder had shocked Europe. Beckett was declared a martyr and canonised and his tomb drew pilgrims to Canterbury until the shrine was destroyed during Henry VIII's reign.

Three Compasses, Cowcross Street EC1 has a sign linking it to the symbol used by carpenters.

The Three Crowns, East Street E1 and the **Three Crowns**, Babmaes Street SW1. Both signs show three crowns as worn by a monarch but there are several interpretations of the name. They may have been the crowns worn by the three Magi but these would become obsolete at the Reformation. When James I became King of England the three crowns referred to the union of England, Scotland and Wales. There may have been a heraldic interpretation referring to the Worshipful Company of Drapers. In east London when a crown coin was worth five shillings, three crowns were fifteen shillings or as the locals preferred to say, fifteen bob. The innocuous crowns noted on the inn sign of the Babmaes Street very small intimate pub might refer to anything.

*Three Compasses, Cowcross Street
EC1*

Three Crowns, Babmaes Street SW1

Three Greyhounds, Greek Street W1. The sign depicts the heads of three greyhounds and refers back to the time when Soho was open country and greyhounds were used as hunting dogs. Although the pub has a half-timbered exterior, the building dates from 1920.

The Three Kings, Clerkenwell Close EC1. Usually this sign, which is one of the oldest in use, depicts the three Magi, Caspar, Melchior and Balthazar who came from the East to visit the Christ child in Bethlehem. This sign is an odd one featuring King Kong, Elvis and Henry VIII while the inside has an eclectic collection of artefacts including Arsenal memorabilia and giant playing cards.

The Three Stags, Kennington Park Road SE1 has a sign with three stags' heads on one side and three stags in different poses on the other. This pub was the boozing place for Charlie Chaplin's father who spent so much money here that he was reduced to poverty and had to place his son in the workhouse. The pub contains references to Charlie Chaplin.

The Three Tuns, Portman Mews West W1 and the **Three Tuns**, Jewry Street EC3 have signs showing three barrels, which are on the arms of the Worshipful Company of Vintners.

The Tipperary, Fleet Street EC1. The sign depicts a farmer wearing white breeches, yellow waistcoat and green coat, smoking a pipe and gazing out over a lush landscape of fields and hills. This pub is said to be the earliest dating from before the Great Fire of London (1666), which survived because it was made of stone. It was originally called the **Boar's Head**, but in 1700, S.G. Mooney & Sons, Dublin Brewers, bought it to convert it into the first Irish pub in London. In 1918 some printers in Fleet Street who had survived the fighting in the First World War renamed the pub the **Tipperary** after the famous song. In the 1960s the pub was refurbished in the style of what it had been in the Mooney days.

Tom Cribb, Panton Street SW1

Tollesbury Barge, Millwall Inner Dock, Marsh Wall E14. This pub is a converted East Coast grain barge, which helped to evacuate troops from Dunkirk in 1940. It was the only Thames barge which escaped being sunk.

Tom Cribb, Panton Street SW1. Tom Cribb was a bare-knuckle boxing champion between 1809 and 1822. His first fight, which was over seventy-six rounds, was in 1805 when he had been retired from the navy. He then became a coal porter at Wapping where he was known as 'The Black Diamond'. The present public house dates from the early 1900s and was named in his honour in 1960. The sign depicts two bare-chested men fighting. The pub is mentioned by Conan Doyle, and also by Thackeray in his novel *Vanity Fair*.

The Tottenham, Oxford Street W1 has had a pub on this site since 1836, although it was called the **Flying Horse** until 1894. It served theatre goers at the nearby Tottenham Court Theatre, one of the best music halls in London.

*The Tower Tavern, Clipstone Street
W1*

Tower Tavern, Clipstone Street W1 most suitably has a sign depicting the Post Office Tower, which is close by.

The Town of Ramsgate, Wapping High Street E1 was originally called the **Red Cow** (not after an animal but after an attractive barmaid) and then the **Prince of Denmark**. It changed its name because many Ramsgate fishermen unloaded their catch on Wapping Old Stairs alongside the pub. The pub sign shows what the port of Ramsgate may have been in the mid-nineteenth century. The very narrow riverside pub is mainly seventeenth and eighteenth century and photographs of old Wapping are displayed on the walls. Press gangs are reputed to have used the pub in the nineteenth century to get men drunk and then press them into service in the navy. The men were held in the cellars until they could be taken on board ships, as also were convicts awaiting transportation. Judge Jeffreys was captured in this pub while attempting to flee the country (*See* the **Prospect of Whitby**). Nearby is Execution Dock. Those who were destined to die were chained to posts in the river and held there until covered by three tides.

Trafalgar Tavern, Park Road SE10. The pub, built in 1837, was named after the battle, which took place in 1805, and provided a home to seamen. In the nineteenth century it was famous for its whitebait suppers, which were attended by senior members of the Liberal party, including Mr Gladstone. The Tories went to the **Ship** (now demolished). In 1915, the pub became a seamen's hostel and then a working men's club. It was finally refurbished and reopened in 1965. The name reflects the fact that Lord Nelson's body lay in state in the Painting Hall, Greenwich before being given a funeral procession along the Thames and buried in St Paul's Cathedral.

The Two Brewers, Monmouth Street WC2. The sign shows two draymen dressed as seventeenth-century workmen carrying a barrel between them on a pole. Draymen usually delivered the beer.

The Two Brewers, Monmouth Street WC2

The Two Chairmen. Two pubs in Dartmouth Street SW1 and Warwick House Street SW1 both display a sign of two men carrying a sedan chair, which was a convenient method of transporting people, especially ladies, in the eighteenth century through London streets when these were extremely muddy. The panel of the chair on the sign in Warwick House Street depicts a royal monogram of two interlocked 'Cs'. Sedan chairs were first introduced into London about 1640. Prince Charles, son of Charles I, and his great friend, the Duke of Buckingham, had been to Spain to woo the daughter of the King of Spain. In this they were unsuccessful but they brought the novel means of transport to London and the popularity of this form of transport lasted until well into the eighteenth century. Many pubs recruited chairmen to carry their drinkers home and these two were amongst the first.

Turners Old Star, Watts Street E1. Joseph Turner (1775-1851), one of the most distinguished of British painters, was fascinated by the river Thames and the life on it. He also had a secret life haunting the streets of Wapping where he is reputed to have had several mistresses, and making erotic sketches. In 1833 he met Sophia Booth from Margate who became his mistress. When he inherited two cottages he converted them to a tavern, naming it **Old Star** and installed Sophia as the landlady. The pub survived in a more dilapidated state until it was refurbished in 1967.

The Turks Head, Motcomb Street SW1. The sign depicts a Turk wearing a blue robe against a background of a mosque. The name is a variation on the Saracen's Head. Turk's heads act as keystones in lower ground windows. The name is derived from a coffee house, which stood here in 1704. In the building Dr Johnson, Sir Joshua Reynolds and James Boswell founded a literary society.

The Tyburn, Edgware Road NW2 is now a modern glass-walled pub with nothing to remind anyone that it was a pub opposite to the place of execution at Tyburn. If there are ghosts on the site they would be scared by the frenzied traffic at the meeting of roads at Marble Arch.

U

The Uxbridge Arms, Uxbridge Street W8. Sign shows a coat of arms of Uxbridge.

V

The Viaduct Tavern, Newgate Street EC1. The signboard depicts Holborn Viaduct constructed by William Heywood in 1867 to cross the waters of the Holebourne. The pub was built in 1869 but stands on the site of part of Newgate Prison so that the cellars are reputed have once been used as cells to house prisoners. In the interior are busts of judges who presided in the Old Bailey. There are marble pillars and some splendid woodcarving. The pictures are representations of the four statues on the viaduct – agriculture, commerce, fine arts and science.

Victoria. The Victoria or Queen Victoria is a very popular name for a pub and the sign can depict the queen in her youth or in her old age. Her long reign (1837-1901) ensured her popularity and after her death the number of pubs bearing her name increased. The **Victoria** in Black Prince Road SE1 has a sign showing the queen as she appeared on the Penny Black stamp. The **Victoria** pub sign in Strathearn Place W2 depicts the queen in her later years. This pub has a bar, which was removed from the Gaiety Theatre in the Strand, and is reputed to have been a haunt of Charles Dickens who once lived in the Bayswater Road. The **Victoria**, Mornington Terrace NW1 has a sign showing the young Queen. (*See* colour picture 29.)

The Victory, High Street, Colliers Wood SW19 has a sign showing the ship in which Lord Nelson died at the Battle of Trafalgar in 1805. The ship is now on permanent display at Portsmouth.

W

The Walrus and the Carpenter, Lower Thames Street EC3. The sign relates to the poem in Lewis Carroll's book, *Alice in Wonderland*. In chapter four, Tweedledee relates to Alice the sad story of how the walrus and the carpenter consumed the oysters that they had invited to, 'a pleasant walk, a pleasant talk, along the briny beach'. This pub used to be known as **The Cock** and was used by fish porters and traders from Billingsgate before the market moved to Docklands.

The Water Rats, Greys Inn Road WC1 was originally the **Pindar of Wakefield**. It was renamed after the Grand Order of Water Rats, founded in 1889, the charity organised by stage entertainers. The charity is presumed to be named after a pony, nicknamed the Water Rat, which belonged to the founder of the charity. The sign shows a shield with entwined initials with two rat supporters.

The Wellesley Arms, Sydney Street SW3. The sign depicts a young Arthur Wellesley before he became first Marquis Wellington and later Duke of Wellington. The pub was built in 1823 and is reputed to have a resident ghost who always makes his own breakfast.

The Wellington, Strand WC1 has a profile of the duke in gold against a black background. The **Wellington at Waterloo** SE1 has has the duke's head between two flags. (*See* the **Duke of Wellington**.)

The Wellesley Arms, Sydney Street SW3

The Wells Tavern, Wells Walk NW3. The discovery of chalybeate waters in 1701 led to them being exploited as a spa by John Duffield. The tavern served the clientele, under several names including the **Green Man** and by 1721 the **White Stone**. The pub was reputed to have a dubious reputation and at one time performed clandestine marriages. It was rebuilt and enlarged by taking in the adjoining house and now serves a respectable clientele.

The Wheatsheaf, Rathbone Place W1. This is usually a rural sign but this one depicts the essentials of life: the wheat sheaf, a loaf of bread, a bottle of beer, and two apples. The **Wheatsheaf**, Storey Street SE1 and the **Wheatsheaf**, Putney Bridge Road SW18 both have a single wheat sheaf. (*See* colour picture 30.)

The White Ferry House, Sutherland Street SW1. Although the sign depicts a white house by a river there seems to be no connection with a ferry. This pub has recently had a makeover to restore it to its Victorian splendour. The mixed collection of prints on the walls is worth studying.

The White Hart was the heraldic device of Richard II (1377-99). The **White Hart**, Kennington Lane SE1 has a sign showing a hart kneeling down, which is reminiscent of one on the diptych of Richard II in the National Gallery. The **White Hart**, Giltspur Street EC1 has the sign of a hart kneeling down with a medieval crown enchained round its neck. The **White Hart**, Drury Lane WC2 claims to be the oldest inn in London, having been first built in 1216. In the **White Hart**, Gunthorpe Street E1, originally Clutterbuck's Ale House dating from 1721, Martha Turner had her last drink before she met her fate with Jack the Ripper. The sign of a standing white hart is above the entrance in Whitechapel Road. (*See* colour picture 31.)

White Horse. There are many inn signs depicting this horse. Originally it was an heraldic device of the Kings of Wessex and a white horse appears on the arms of the county of Kent. Occasionally a horse is on the arms of some City of London Livery Guilds for example the Carmen and the Coachmen. The Royal House of Hanover had the symbol of a galloping white horse and in the eighteenth century, when George I (1714-27) ascended the English throne it became politic to display loyalty to the new regime. Today, signs mainly depict a horse and its artistic value depends on the signs. The **White Horse** in Brewer Street W1 shows a handsome white horse standing in a river. This pub was rebuilt in 1930 in Art Deco style. The **White Horse & Bower**, Horseferry Road SW1 depicts a rather stocky horse standing against some trees. The **White Horse** in Newburgh Street W1 has a more modern sign showing a horse sitting on its rear haunches with what appears to be a blue fan spreading above it. The **White Horse**, Fleet Road

NW3 shows a rider guiding a white horse. The **White Horse**, Hoxton Street N1, even though a simple pub, has an elaborate sign showing a rearing horse with a collar round the neck with a long chain. In heraldic terms this is 'a horse crined and unguled argent, with a coronet of crosses paty and fleurs-de-lis, a chain affixed thereto'.

The White Lion, James Street WC1 is a pub in the heart of Covent Garden. The white lion was the heraldic sign of Edward IV or the Dukes of Norfolk. The pub has a splendid cut out sign of a lion rampant.

The White Lion, James Street WC1

Above left: *The White Swan, Alie Street E1*

Above right: *The White Swan and Cuckoo, Wapping Lane E1*

The White Swan, Alie Street E1. White and black swans are common inn signs and are seen in a variety of heraldic coats of arms. A white swan was the badge of Edward II, Henry IV and Edward IV. This particular sign represents a swan swimming gently on a river. There are variations such as the **White Swan & Cuckoo**, Wapping Lane E1 where the whimsical sign has the swan placing its wing in a friendly fashion over the shoulder of the cuckoo. The **White Swan**, Fetter Lane EC4 has a minimalist sign of a large beak against a white background.

Widow's Son, Devon Road E3

The Whitesmiths Arms, Crosby Row SE1 commemorates a tinsmith or smith who worked in silver and other valuable metals. It might also indicate those who polished and finished the product.

Widow's Son, Devons Road E3. This unique pub (also known as the **Bun House**) has the story depicted on the sign. A widow, whose son left to go to sea, asked his mother to bake a hot cross bun for him when he returned. His mother baked a huge bun for him on Good Friday, but as he was lost at sea he never returned. The widow, in desperate hope, continued to bake a hot cross bun every year until she died stringing them in her kitchen on a cord. Later her cottage was demolished and a pub built on the site. The tradition was continued, placing the buns in a net above the bar.

Today flags and hats given by seamen decorate the bar. A fire some years ago destroyed the collection of buns apart from a few which were saved and in their charcoal state they hang still above the bar. Every Good Friday, in the midst of great celebrations, a young seaman places a bun in the net. A poem by Harold Adshead tells the tale and ends, 'The buns hang high for all to see, a blackened mass above, a truly strange epitome, of patient motherhood'. According to an ancient superstition buns made on Good Friday will never grow stale and if ground up can be used as a medicine.

William IV, Shepherdess Walk N1. A Victorian working men's pub displaying the arms of William IV (1830-37) set within the Order of the Garter.

Williamson's Tavern, Groveland Court EC4

Williamson's Tavern, Groveland Court, Off Bow Lane EC4. This well-hidden pub, once the residence of Sir John Fastolf, was rebuilt after the 1666 Great Fire to become the residence of the Lord Mayor of London. Numerous important personages were entertained here, including William and Mary who are reputed to have presented the wrought iron gates. In 1753 Robert Williamson bought the property and converted it into Williamson's Hotel. It was rebuilt as a pub in 1932 and the fireplace was built from Roman tiles found 10ft below the present ground surface.

The Windmill, Clapham Common SW4. The pub is named after a windmill, which probably existed in the seventeenth century and stood here until the twentieth century. The pub was built to serve the millers, who grew their wheat in what was once farmland. This pub can be identified in J.F. Herring's painting, *Returning from the Derby* which hangs in the Tate Gallery. There is a print of this in one of the bars. The **Windmill**, Windmill Street W1 ignores its urban surroundings and opts for a sign showing a mill set in the open countryside, as does that of the **Windmill**, Tabernacle Street EC1, where the miller stands in the open doorway.

The Windsor, New London Street EC3. The sign depicts two guards on duty either side of the gates of the castle, which is seen in the background. On the round tower flies the Royal Standard.

The Windsor Castle, Campden Hill Road W8, built in 1835 is said to have received its name from the fact that Windsor Castle could be seen from here. The sign is a splendid one showing Windsor Castle and the Thames. The **Windsor Castle**, Lanark Place W1 is an unpretentious pub with a sign showing a handsome view of the castle across the Thames. The **Windsor Castle**, Crawford Place W1 has a sentry box in which is a model soldier guardsman. Inside is a motley collection of objects.

The Witness Box, Tudor Street EC4 has a sign showing a somewhat nervous witness as he gives evidence from the witness box. This is in

The Witness Box, Tudor Street EC4

The Windsor, New London Street EC3

The World's End, Camden
High Street NW1

a street leading to the temple and the annual 'Witness Box Awards' for the best crime writer's reporting account of the year used to be held here.

The Woodbine, Blackstock Road N4 has a sign showing this twining flower.

Woodin's Shades, Bishopsgate EC2. This pub gets its name from William Woodin who bought the business in 1863. The term 'shades' refers to wine vaults with drinking bars shaded by being either below ground or covered with an awning. The sign shows the vaults with several barrels and two barmen siphoning off the ale from the cask to a tub.

The World's End, Kings Road SW10. The name was often used to indicate an isolated inn or one which stood on a road leading out of an inhabited area, which might have once been the case here as this area of Chelsea is known as World's End although now it is now nowhere near the edge of London. This huge pub, built about 1900, replaced an earlier one built in the eighteenth century. The **World's End**, Camden High Street NW1 has a sign showing a small ship, seemingly crewed by Vikings, going over the edge of the sea.

The World Turned Upside Down, New Kent Road SE1. The reference is found in the *Bible* (Acts 17:6) when the Jews sought out Paul and Silas, who were preaching, crying 'those that have turned the world upside down have come hither'. The signs here, both of which have gone, were more prosaic. The first depicted a man walking at the South Pole. The next on one side depicted a fish hooking an angler out of the water and on the other a football kicking a man into the goal net.

The Wrestlers, North Road N6. The inn sign shows one man about to throw the other over his shoulder. Over the fireplace is a set of antlers which refers to an old ceremony of 'swearing on the horns', which takes place here and at one time in other surrounding pubs. This dates back to the seventeenth century and any stranger to the area who drinks at the pub is asked to swear a comic oath. Details are placed on the wall.

Y

Ye Grapes, Shepherd Market W1, rebuilt in 1882, began as the Market Coffee House and served the May Fair, which took place in the area giving its name to the district. It is not enough that the sign outside has a bunch of grapes; the theme is repeated in the carvings inside. Shepherd Market owes its origin to Edward Shepherd who bought the site of the annual May Fair held from 1688 to 1708 and then banned because of disgraceful behaviour by the clientele. He began building houses and shops in 1735 thereby creating the interesting enclave it remains to this day. This is one of the few pubs that actively encourage people to bring in their own food while enjoying a drink.

Ye Old Red Cow, Long Lane EC1. The sign showing the cow is appropriate as the pub is the venue for porters at nearby Smithfield market.

Ye Old White Horse, Sheffield Street WC1. The sign shows a huge white shire horse with decorated mane standing quietly held by the farmer.

Ye Olde Cheshire Cheese, Fleet Street EC4. Although extended and refurbished this pub can claim to be one of the oldest genuine survivors in the City of London, having been rebuilt after the 1666 Great Fire. Built first in 1558, it was a favourite pub of Samuel

Johnson and numerous notable writers: Voltaire (then in exile), Dickens, Thackeray, Conan Doyle, Yeats and George Bernard Shaw. Samuel Johnson, who lived in a nearby court, was a frequent visitor. One of its specialities was to serve beef puddings, which contained beef, mushrooms, oysters, kidneys and even larks. These, boiled in a huge copper, could weigh up to 8olbs.

Ye Olde Cock Tavern, Fleet Street EC4, opened in 1888, contains fittings from the former branch of the Bank of England almost opposite. The original **Cock Tavern** was knocked down in 1887 on the opposite side of the road to build the Law Courts Branch of the Bank of England. It was mentioned by the diarist Samuel Pepys when, in April 1668 he went, 'to the Cock alehouse to drink and eat a lobster and sang, and mighty merry'. A fire in 1990 destroyed many of the old fittings but some Dickens memorabilia remains on the second floor.

Ye Olde London, Ludgate Hill EC4 has a sign showing the griffin, mythical beast of the City of London with a shield of the city arms. In the cellars are parts of the Roman wall of London which makes its way under Ludgate Hill towards the river.

Ye Olde Mitre Tavern, Ely Court EC1. The sign depicts the headgear worn by a bishop or abbot and is the symbol of his office. The pub, according to the sign, dates from 1546, but was rebuilt in the late eighteenth century, at the same time as the Bishop of Ely's town house was demolished. It owes its name to the fact that it is on land once owned by the Bishop of Ely being originally built as an inn to house the bishop's servants. The alleyway leads from Hatton Gardens to Ely Place where the bishop's town house stood. Part of the land was leased to Sir Thomas Hatton who gave his name to Hatton Street, now the London centre of the jewelry retailing industry. One curiosity is that in the bar is part of a cherry tree trunk around which Elizabeth I is reputed to have danced when she visited Sir Christopher Hatton, who inherited the house nearby. Another

Ye Olde Mitre Tavern, Ely Court EC1

is that technically the pub is still part of Cambridgeshire where the bishop's diocese was situated and until the nineteenth century the pub license was granted by Cambridge magistrates. Until recently the City of London police had no jurisdiction there.

Ye Olde Spotted Horse, High Street SW15 was originally called the **Blue Anchor** in the eighteenth century. Later, when it was given its present name it was given a sign of a wooden spotted horse, which still survives.

Ye Olde Watling, Watling Street EC4. The sign shows a paved road, purporting to be Roman as a Roman soldier stands on it. The pub stands on the original Watling Street which was constructed by the Romans as one of the first roads leading from the Roman port of Richborough and continuing through London to Wroxeter, the Roman Uriconium, and a road becoming later the A5. The pub, which used brine picked lengths of timber from old ships of war, also has the distinction of being one of few surviving houses being built after the Great Fire of London in 1666 by Sir Christopher Wren who used it as an office while he worked on St Paul's Cathedral. It was remodelled in 1901.

Ye Olde White Bear, Well Road NW3 is a local pub well used by actors and writers who have scrawled on the walls. The white bear, displayed on the pub sign, was a heraldic device used by the Earls of Kent. Sir Francis Drake's fleet also had a ship named thus, which took part in the siege of Cadiz in 1563.

Ye Olde Watling, Watling Street EC4

Ye Three Lords, Minories EC3. This pub has no sign but its name deserves a comment. The lords are the last to have been executed on Tower Hill, this being for their part in the attempt to restore Prince Charles Edward Stuart to the English throne in the rebellion of the highland clans in 1745. The rebellion was defeated at the Battle of Culloden in 1746 and the lords were brought south for incarceration in the Tower of London and their later execution. The lords were Lord Balmerino, the Earl of Kilmarnock and Lord Lovat, the last men to be beheaded publicly in Britain.

The York, Islington High Street N1. Until the eighteenth century the area was open countryside, part of land owned by the Patten and Rhodes families. In 1838 James Patten owned land in the area now known as Duncan Street and had a private house on the site. In 1851 this became the York Hotel. It was rebuilt in 1872 and retains its Victorian interior. The sign displays the white rose of York.

Yorkshire Grey, Theobalds Road WC1. This was a famous breed of shire horses, which were once used for ploughing. The pub dates back to 1822 and there is a model of a horse's head over the door. According to a notice on the wall, the name could refer to a horse used by soldiers in the city and it was certainly bred to carry a man in armour on horseback. It could also be a fighting cock and a grey racehorse called Isaac, unbeaten for nearly two decades in Yorkshire. A fourth reference is to a coaching horse and this may be noted on the sign of the **Yorkshire Grey**, Langham Street W1 where a trim horse draws a carriage. (*See* colour picture 32.)

Z

The Zetland Arms, Bute Street SW7. The sign has the coat of arms, with lion supporters, of the Marquis of Zetland, argent, a lion rampant gules within a double tressure flory counterflory, all within a bordure azure.

The Zetland Arms, Bute Street SW7

Other local titles published by Tempus

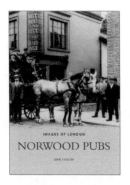

Norwood Pubs

JOHN COULTER

During the Victorian period there was an explosion
in the number of newly-built pubs and hotels in
the London suburb of Norwood. Containing over
100 illustrations, this fascinating book captures
the architecture of Norwood's Dickensian pubs,
revealing each establishment's history. It will prove
an informative and entertaining guide for anyone
interested in the history of brewing.

07524 3837 9

Old Kent Inns

DONALD STUART

The old inns of Kent have a rich history: containing
more than 90 photographs, this fascinating book tells
of spy-holes and smugglers, of cock-fighting, ghosts,
buried treasure, murders and hanging, of escaped
convicts and Siamese twins, phantom ships, hidden
tunnels, hiding places and bodies bricked into walls.
This fascinating book takes the reader on a journey
from Acol all the way to Yalding.

07524 3959 6

City of Westminster

BRIAN GIRLING

This collection of old photographs of one of Britain's best-known areas recalls the Edwardian period of London's old City of Westminster. Using over 200 images, this volume leads the reader around Pimlico through Belgravia and Knightsbridge, Mayfair and St James' and on to Soho and the West End's famous theatreland. *City of Westminster* and will appeal to all who know the area.

978 07524 3191 9

Greenwich Centre of the World

DAVID RAMZAN

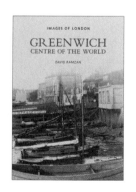

Greenwich has always been well known for its position on the meridian line, however as David Ramzan illustrates in this new book, the area has a rich history with its commercial and industrial businesses in the town or on the river and its naval and military connections. Illustrated with over 200 images, the book brings to life bygone days when Greenwich was a major tourist attraction.

978 07524 4260 0

If you are interested in purchasing other books published by Tempus, or in case you
have difficulty finding any Tempus books in your local bookshop, you can also place
orders directly through our website

www.tempus-publishing.com